Rose Elliot's
ZODIAC
COOKBOOK

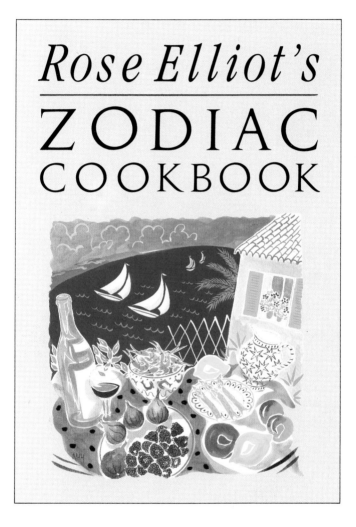

Rose Elliot's
ZODIAC
COOKBOOK

Fabulous recipes for every star sign

PYRAMID BOOKS

ABOUT THE INGREDIENTS
All the recipes in this book are vegetarian.
Wholefood ingredients are used for preference, although
treats and gifts include the occasional indulgence such as
white flour, sugar and chocolate. Eggs are always
free range and of standard size.

First published in 1989
by Pyramid
an imprint of the Octopus Publishing Group,
Michelin House, 81 Fulham Road,
London SW3 6RB.

ISBN 1 871 307 961

Produced by Mandarin Offset. Printed and bound in Hong Kong

CONTENTS

INTRODUCTION

If you know your Sun sign, and those of your friends and relatives, you are in a very good position to know what they like to eat, what they ought to eat, and what would please them in the way of edible gifts.

The sign of the Zodiac under which we are born determines character, physical type and health, plus attitudes to food, drink, cooking and entertaining. Each sign has its own clearly defined personality, strong and weak points, likes and dislikes. These extend to the types of food preferred, how it is cooked and how and when it is eaten.

Some signs, for instance Taurus and Cancer, are naturally drawn to food. Others, such as Gemini, Aquarius and Pisces are more interested in ideas and conversation, while a third group, including Aries and Sagittarius, regard food as fuel, to stock them up for their active, racy life-style.

Hot, spicy foods are preferred by some, including Scorpio. Others, of which Libra is the supreme example, adore sweet and creamy foods. The person who treats a dinner party like a stage production, and who loves stunning guests with dramatic dishes, is likely to be a Leo. Conversely, there are the practical perfectionists, Virgo and Capricorn, who will take pains over the details. Virgoan guests probably know all the nutrients in the food and may well infuriate the host (or their mother!) by picking all the peas out of their casserole.

The suggestions in this book are based upon my own observations of the character and likes and dislikes of the signs of the Zodiac, and of the nature of the planets with which each sign is associated. In this context, I have used well-established astrological principles. I have also drawn on the work of the 17th-century astrologer and herbalist, Nicholas Culpeper, who analysed British herbs, fruit and vegetables according to their essential nature and then classified them under the seven planets which were known at that time.

BASIC ASTROLOGY

During the year, as the Earth orbits the Sun, the Sun appears against 12 successive starry backgrounds, the constellations, each relating to one sign of the Zodiac. In early spring it is seen against Aries, then against Taurus, and so on. The exact day and time when it makes the transit from one sign to another, incidentally, varies from year to year because of the effect of leap years. That is why the dates given in magazine horoscopes sometimes vary. To know for sure which sign you are, if you were born around the change-over dates or on the 'cusp', as astrologers say, you need to get an astrologer to look up your date and year in an ephemeris or have your horoscope professionally calculated. If the Sun changed signs on your actual birthday, the exact time of your birth will determine your Sun sign.

Rising Signs
You may say: 'Geminians are not supposed to take

much interest in food. I'm a Geminian and I absolutely adore it, so astrology must be wrong.'

This is not necessarily so. Although Sun signs are what most people know about, there is in fact a great deal more to astrology than that.

When astrologers draw up a horoscope, or birth-chart, we look at the sign in which each of the planets is placed, not just the Sun. The other planets are constantly moving round the Sun, so are seen against different signs of the Zodiac too. If you have your horoscope drawn up, the exact positions of all the planets at your moment of birth are calculated and entered into your birth chart. (Astrologers, for simplicity, refer to the Sun and Moon as planets, although they know that this is not astronomically the correct term.)

Apart from the Sun, the factor which probably has the most effect on your character is the rising sign or Ascendant. That is the sign of the Zodiac which was rising above the eastern horizon at the time and place of your birth.

While the Earth's yearly orbit around the Sun gives us the passage of the Sun through the signs of the Zodiac, it is the Earth's other motion, spinning on its axis every 24 hours, which dictates the rising sign. The rising sign is the sign which, because of the Earth's motion, appears to be coming up over the horizon.

This is easy to understand if you imagine you are watching the Sun rise. As the Sun comes up over the horizon, behind it, although invisible to you, is the starry sign of the astrological Zodiac in which it is placed. So if you were watching the Sun rise in early April, the astrological sign of Aries would also be rising. A baby born at that place and at that time would have Aries as its rising sign, giving an unusually enthusiastic, impulsive, warm-hearted nature.

However, the Sun moves on, together with its starry background, or sign of the Zodiac. An hour or two later both it and Aries would have moved well up above the horizon and the next sign of the astrological Zodiac, Taurus, would be rising. A child born at that time would have the Sun in Aries and Taurus rising, and would have quite a different personality. With Arien drive and energy moderated by the practicality and determination of Taurus, this child would really go places.

At noon, with the Sun at zenith, the sign of Taurus would have moved well up over the horizon, as would the next sign, Gemini. Had Gemini been rising when the baby was born, it would have given a child who expressed the Arien drive and adventurousness in lively, communicative ways, as a journalist, perhaps. At noon, however, Cancer would be rising, giving a very creative, sensitive, restless personality, with a conflict between the independence and self-centredness of Aries and the dependency and caring of Cancer.

A baby born later in the afternoon, when the next sign, Leo is rising, would have all the warmth and spontaneity of Aries reinforced by the similar qualities of Leo, and would be particularly energetic and creative, rather impulsive and inclined to take on too much; quite different from a child born even later in the afternoon, with Virgo rising. Here, the Aries drive would be harnessed to great intelligence to achieve practical goals. Aries' impulsiveness would be greatly moderated by the cool, careful, cautious qualities of Virgo.

When the Sun sets, the sign of Aries, too, would be slipping down below the western horizon, and the opposite sign of the Zodiac, Libra, would be rising, giving a lively, sociable, forceful yet charming personality with possible musical gifts. Then Scorpio would be rising, overlaying the enthusiasm and adventurousness of Aries with emotional intensity and secretiveness and increasing the determination. Two hours later, the next rising sign, Sagittarius, would give a personality like that of the Sun in Aries and Leo rising, with warmth, impulsiveness and vigour all accentuated. This combination would result in a particularly independent and freedom-loving individual, most likely rather sporty.

Capricorn rising, around midnight, would give a character similar to that of the Sun in Aries and Taurus rising, with the practicality, self-discipline and common sense of Capricorn holding the restlessness and enthusiasm of Aries in check. This would give a particularly strong personality with great potential for achievement. In the early hours of the following day, a child born with the next sign (Aquarius) rising, would be particularly self-sufficient, with the Arien energy expressing itself in idiosyncratic ways. This child would be a thinker,

perhaps an inventor, bringing a stamp of individuality to everything he did. The baby born just before sunrise, with Pisces rising, would have the Arien forcefulness blurred by the sensitivity and restlessness of Pisces. This child would have plenty of ideas but, unless there were other more practical factors in the horoscope, would have difficulty in making use of them. He might be a born actor, or particularly good with people.

All the signs rise during the course of the day, but because the earth spins at an angle on its axis, so that the ecliptic is viewed, from Earth's point of view, at an oblique angle, some signs take longer to rise than others, as a bigger chunk of them is exposed (like slicing a cucumber slant-wise instead of straight down). So while some signs take only around an hour to rise, others take nearly three hours. If you were born during one of the quick signs, and the midwife was slow to note the time of your birth, you could end up with the wrong rising sign! So it is very important that a baby's moment of birth is recorded exactly – to the nearest minute.

If you know your rising sign, you will probably recognize as much of yourself in the descriptions and food likes of this sign as of those of your Sun sign. If you don't know your rising sign, you can have this worked out for you. It will probably give you many interesting insights into your personality generally as well as your attitude to diet and health.

I think I identify about 60 per cent with my Sun sign and 40 per cent with my rising sign; but I also recognize preferences which can be attributed to other aspects of my horoscope. The other planets, particularly the Moon, planet of nurture, of early conditioning and habits, and Venus, planet of pleasure, have a bearing on the foods we like, although the influence of the Sun and rising signs are much stronger.

THE SIGNS OF THE ZODIAC

The 12 signs of the Zodiac are always listed in their calendar order, starting with Aries.

Aries is taken as the starting point because the Sun's entry into this sign coincides with the Vernal equinox.

SIGN	SYMBOL
Aries	the ram
Taurus	the bull
Gemini	the twins
Cancer	the crab
Leo	the lion
Virgo	the virgin
Libra	the scales
Scorpio	the scorpion
Sagittarius	the archer
Capricorn	the goat
Aquarius	the man with the watering pot
Pisces	the fishes

An easy way to remember the order of the signs is this old rhyme:

> The ram, the bull, the heavenly twins,
> Next the crab, the lion shines,
> The virgin and the scales,
> The scorpion, archer and the goat,
> The man who bears the watering pot,
> And the fish with the glittering tails.

The Zodiac signs are divided into two groups known as the Elements and Qualities. These are related to the essential nature of the signs, and signs belonging to the same group share the same attitudes. The elements and the signs which belong to them are as follows.

The Elements

Fire Aries, Leo and Sagittarius. These signs are all by nature warm, outgoing, impulsive, ready to try new things, to initiate new schemes, to have a bit of a gamble. They live at a fast pace and have plenty of vitality, and they see food as a source of energy.

Earth Taurus, Virgo, Capricorn. These are the down-to-earth, practical signs. They are realistic, businesslike and inclined to be conventional. Essentially cautious, their pace is naturally slower than that of the fire signs, and they appreciate food and comfort.

Air Gemini, Libra, Aquarius. This is the intellectual set. They reason things out and are not swayed by their emotions. They are sociable and communicative, highly strung and quick in their thought and movements. They are more interested in ideas and conversation than food and practical matters.

Water Cancer, Scorpio, Pisces. These individuals are guided by the heart and emotions rather than the head. They are sensitive to atmosphere and the feelings of others. Naturally sympathetic, they are sensitive to the moods of others and adapt easily to the prevailing environment and company. Food is important to them, for comfort as much as flavour.

There is a natural affinity between the Fire and Air signs and between the Earth and Water signs. People born under the Fire and Air signs are more outgoing, extrovert and ideas-orientated than those born under the more introvert Earth and Water signs. Earth and Water individuals tend to be concerned with feelings and practical matters and their pace tends to be slower than that of the Fire and Air people.

Qualities

In addition to grouping by element, the signs of the Zodiac are categorized according to their quality. The qualities are Cardinal, Fixed and Mutable. They describe the way in which the signs act.

Cardinal signs Aries, Cancer, Libra, Capricorn. These are the signs which usher in the four seasons. They behave in an active, initiatory way. Those born under them are outgoing types. They like action and their strength lies in starting projects, although they are not so good at maintaining these for long periods of time. Those with most of their planets in Cardinal signs will be forceful and energetic. The Cardinal signs give qualities of leadership.

Fixed signs Taurus, Leo, Scorpio, Aquarius. These are the signs which like to maintain the status quo. Those born under them are determined individuals with great willpower. Once they have made up their minds to achieve an aim, they are not easily diverted. In fact they can hold on too long, resisting change and stagnating. They are stable and reliable, but need to remain flexible. The Fixed quality tends to give feelings which go very deep but are not always expressed.

Mutable signs Gemini, Virgo, Sagittarius, Pisces. There's no danger of stagnation here! These are the changeable signs and people born under them find it easy to adapt to the circumstance or mood of the moment. They bend easily in the wind and then bounce back again. They love variety, are open to ideas and possibilities, and tend to move restlessly from one interest or project to another. The Mutable signs are not good at finishing things – they are too easily diverted by something new, and the Mutable quality gives an active brain and a tendency towards cerebral interests.

Each of the Elements (Fire, Earth, Air and Water) is expressed in each of the three Qualities (Cardinal, Fixed and Mutable). So, for instance, in the Fire Signs Cardinal Fire is Aries, Fixed Fire is Leo and Mutable Fire is Sagittarius.

	CARDINAL	FIXED	MUTABLE
FIRE	Aries	Leo	Sagittarius
EARTH	Capricorn	Taurus	Virgo
AIR	Libra	Aquarius	Gèmini
WATER	Cancer	Scorpio	Pisces

It is interesting to see how the attributes of the Element and Quality mix to express the personality of the signs. The Fire element, for instance, is always warm, enthusiastic and extrovert. The Cardinal quality, which is rather similar, being active, energetic and outgoing, intensifies these characteristics to give the ardent, adventurous personality of Aries.

This is very different from the Cardinal quality in its Earth expression, where the activity, energy and qualities of leadership are channelled in practical ways to give the hardworking, ambitious, success-orientated Capricorn temperament. Equally, the Cardinal expression of Fire, as expressed in the directness and independence of Aries can be compared to the Fixed expression of Fire, in the sign of Leo, where the warmth is more controlled and expressed in generosity, creativity and managerial skills; and in Sagittarius, where the Mutable expression gives restlessness, burning desire for freedom and an active brain.

By considering the combined effects of the Element and the Quality of each sign it is possible to build up a picture of the essential characteristics. These can be amplified further by looking at the symbol of the sign, which shows important aspects of it, and by a knowledge of the planet that is said to rule the sign.

THE PLANETS

Each sign is linked with a planet with whose characteristics it has affinity, and that planet is known as the ruling planet.

SIGN	RULING PLANET
Aries	Mars
Taurus	Venus
Gemini	Mercury
Cancer	Moon
Leo	Sun
Virgo	Mercury
Libra	Venus
Scorpio	Mars, Pluto
Sagittarius	Jupiter
Capricorn	Saturn
Aquarius	Saturn, Uranus
Pisces	Jupiter, Neptune

These rulerships date back to ancient times, with the exception of the planets beyond Saturn, which were unknown then. Through examination of the astrological characteristics of these planets, modern astrologers now consider them as co-rulers, Uranus of Aquarius,

Neptune of Pisces and Pluto of Scorpio. Apart from the extra-Saturnian planets and the Sun and the Moon, each planet rules two signs; and three of the signs, Scorpio, Aquarius and Pisces, each have two rulers.

Whereas the signs of the Zodiac represent modes of expression, the planets in the horoscope symbolize basic life-energies. These energies are moulded by the sign of the Zodiac in which they are placed. That is why the basic energy of the Sun, which shows the essential life force, the creative heart of the individual, is different according to its sign. Sun in Aries is different from Sun in Taurus which is different from Sun in Gemini, but all of them represent the life-force of that individual.

The Moon symbolizes emotional response and nurturing ability, and this too varies according to which sign the Moon is placed in in the horoscope. Moon in Aries, for instance, gives quickly roused, very ardent emotions and a great need for independence; Moon in Taurus gives stable emotions and the ability to care for others in practical ways; Moon in Gemini gives changeable but somewhat cool emotions; Moon in Cancer gives very active feelings and much sensitivity, with a need to nurture and be nurtured.

The Moon in Leo gives warm feelings and a tendency to exaggerate the emotions, to overwhelm others and to expect a great deal in return. Moon in Virgo gives shyness and a tendency to repress feelings, with the ability to care for others in very practical ways but a tendency to worry too much, while the Moon in Libra gives a great need for harmony, a liking for company with a certain degree of detachment and a tendency to mood swings. Moon in Scorpio gives intense, deep feelings which are seldom completely expressed. This is coupled with fierce loyalty, also possessiveness. The Moon in Sagittarius gives a rather carefree, happy-go-lucky nature, with a tendency to be restless and to balk against restrictions. Moon in Capricorn, like Moon in Virgo, tends to repress the feelings, which should be expressed as often as possible, and gives strong feelings of responsibility in the care of others. Moon in Aquarius gives an independent spirit with detachment, the ability to stand aside from the feelings, plus a tendency to let others do their own thing, while Moon in Pisces, like Moon in Cancer and Scorpio, is highly sensitive, imaginative, open to every hurt as well as every joy, constantly changing in mood, and kind and caring though somewhat inconsistent in its care of others.

The other life-energies shown by the planets include the ability to relate to others socially and in terms of love. This is symbolized by Venus, and modified by the sign in which Venus is placed. Drive, energy and assertiveness are shown by Mars and its sign; while mental ability and powers of communication are shown by Mercury and its sign. Then there is the ability to expand and find freedom, which is shown by Jupiter and its sign; and the ability to control, discipline and be practical, shown by Saturn and its sign. The outer planets are less personal in effect but their positions in the horoscope show where inner growth, change, aspirations, and transformation are likely to occur.

What is particularly interesting about the symbolism of the planets is that once you understand the basic life-energy shown, you can see it working throughout all aspects of life, from the largest concept to the smallest details, and on physical, mental, emotional and spiritual levels. This is clearly demonstrated by a brief considera-tion of the characteristics of the planets.

By ancient astrological tradition, foods and herbs, as well as other aspects of life, were designated to the various planets. Foods which had the same quality as that of the planet were said to come under the rulership of that planet, since they were in their own way an

expression of it. Thus, for instance, fiery, dry foods such as chilli peppers were said to come under the rulership of fiery, dry Mars. Likewise, cucumbers and courgettes, and other vegetables which are moist and cooling, come under the Moon, which shares these qualities.

These classifications were recorded by the herbalist and astrologer, Nicholas Culpeper (1616-1654) who wrote a number of books including *The Astrological Judgement of Diseases, from the Decumbiture of the Sick,* and *The British Herbal and Family Physician for the Use of Private Families.*

Here are the characteristics of the planets and how these manifest themselves, including their relationship to fruits, vegetables, flowers, nuts and grains.

PLANET	QUALITY
SUN	hot and dry; vibrant, life-giving
MOON	cold and wet; reflective, changing
MERCURY	cold and dry; linking, flexible
VENUS	warm and moist; harmonious, pleasurable
MARS	hot and dry; fiery, incisive
JUPITER	hot and moist; expansive
SATURN	cold and dry; binding, restrictive
URANUS	cold and dry; changing suddenly, surprising
NEPTUNE	cold and moist; nebulous, confusing
PLUTO	cold, dry; transforming, penetrating

The Sun (rules Leo)

At the most physical level, the Sun is the centre of the solar system, around which all the other planets revolve, and is essential to the life of the solar system. In the physical body the Sun symbolizes the centre and life-force, the heart; also the nucleus of each cell. In the world it symbolizes the king, the president or the one with the power. In the home it shows the head of the house, traditionally male, of course. At work it shows the boss. The quality of the Sun is hot and dry, its colours all shades of gold.

Many of the ingredients designated as belonging to the Sun reflect these colours; so we find marigolds and saffron, both of which, according to Culpeper, 'strengthen the heart exceedingly', while saffron also 'quicketh the brain'; and peonies, 'an herb of the sun, and under the Lion'. Also placed under the Sun is rosemary, of which Culpeper says: 'By the warm and comforting heat thereof it helpeth all cold diseases ... the flowers and conserve made of them are singular good to comfort the heart ...'. Other herbs of the Sun are bay, which 'resisteth witchcraft very potently, as also all the evils old Saturn can do the body of man, and they are not a few ...'; also camomile 'because it cured ague ... it taketh away weariness, easeth pains to what parts soever they be applied ...' and angelica which is 'an herb of the sun in Leo, let it be gathered when he is there, the Moon applying to his good aspect ... In all diseases caused by Saturn, that is as good a preservative as grows ...'. Burnet, 'a friend of the heart, liver, and other principal parts of man's body', is also linked with the Sun. Culpeper tells us that 'two or three of the stalks with the leaves put into a cup of wine, especially claret, are known to quicken the spirits, refresh and clear the heart, and drive away melancholy'. Lovage is placed under both the Sun and Taurus, and as for juniper, 'this admirable solar shrub is scarce to be paralleled for its virtues. It is a most admirable counter poison, and as great resistor of the pestilence as any growing: they are excellent good against the bitings of venomous beasts.' Culpeper also puts the ash and the walnut tree, and thus walnuts, under the Sun. Culpeper does not mention them, but I would add to this list, obviously, sunflowers and sunflower seeds and also oranges and all citrus fruits, on account of their colour.

The Moon (rules Cancer)

The Moon, receiver and reflector of light from the Sun, constantly changing in its monthly cycle, symbolizes the feminine principle throughout life. In the horoscope it shows the mother, women and the home; and, as I've already mentioned, it also represents our emotional nature, the kind of nurture we have received and our own ability to nurture.

In the body the Moon is linked with the lymphatic system, the stomach, womb and breasts. The quality of the Moon is said to be cold and wet, and the fruits and vegetables traditionally associated with this planet echo this theme. Traditionally placed under the Moon are cucumbers, which Culpeper calls 'excellent good for a hot stomach and hot liver', melons and lettuces, which 'cool and moisten what heat and dryness Mars causeth'. Courgettes and marrows would also come into this category. Cauliflowers, with their moon-faces, and all cabbages and other brassicas come under the Moon, together with watercress, which Culpeper describes as 'more powerful to cleanse the blood and humours than brook-lime'. Daisies, willow trees, wallflowers, water-lilies, white roses, poppies and poppy seeds are also lunar. Astrologers also place milk and milk products such as curds and cheeses under the Moon, and I would add soya bean curd, or tofu, as well.

Mercury (rules Gemini and Virgo)

Named after the messenger of the gods in ancient mythology, Mercury correlates with the principle of adaptability, changeability, interaction between two parties, intelligence, swiftness and communication. Messengers, agents, writers, students, lecturers and communicators of all kinds are under the rulership of Mercury. In the body, Mercury rules the brain, the motor nerves, speech and hearing organs.

According to astrological tradition, the nature of Mercury is cold and dry, although it takes on the condition around it, so can vary. Herbs and vegetables which come under Mercury, and thus the two signs which it rules, Gemini and Virgo, are carrots, celery and fennel; also hazelnuts, dill and caraway, which Culpeper describes as 'pleasant and comfortable to the stomach'. Other herbs include marjoram, 'warming and comfortable in diseases of the head, stomach, sinews and other parts'; parsley which is 'very comfortable in the stomach' and summer and winter savory which you should 'keep dry by you all the year if you love yourself and your ease'. Mulberries come under Mercury, also ferns, lily of the valley, honeysuckle and lavender.

Venus (rules Taurus and Libra)

Venus is the planet of beauty and of love. Its principle is harmony, pleasure and ease. In life it correlates with young women, lovers, money, art, music and enjoyment. People involved with the worlds of beauty, cosmetics, perfume, interior decoration, art and fashion are symbolized by Venus. In an individual horoscope the position of Venus shows artistic gifts and appreciation, love, relationships and money. It also shows our ability to enjoy ourselves and the activities which we are likely to find pleasurable. In the body, Venus rules the kidneys, veins and glandular secretions.

Many delicious fruits and vegetables come under the rulership of Venus. The list includes apples, pears, apricots and peaches. Culpeper says of the last mentioned that they 'opposeth the ill effects of Mars; and indeed for children and young people nothing is better to purge choler and jaundice than the leaves and flowers of this tree, being made into a syrup or conserve.' Cherries and blackberries are fruits of Venus. So are gooseberries, 'good to stir up a fainting or delayed appetite . . . you may keep them preserved with sugar all year long.' Raspberries and strawberries 'cool the liver, the blood, and the spleen, or an hot choleric stomach', according to Culpeper. They also 'refresh and comfort the fainting spirit and quench thirst'. The vine and its fruits, elderflowers and elderberries, wheat, peas, endive, sorrel, beans and parsnips which 'nourisheth much, and is good and wholesome, but a little windy' also belong to Venus. Jerusalem artichokes are also 'under the dominion of Venus and therefore no marvel if they provoke lust, as indeed they do, being somewhat windy meat'. So says Culpeper.

Of the herbs, there are thyme ('so harmless you need

not fear the use of it'), lovage, burdock and mint ('applied to the forehead and temples, it easeth the pains in the head'). Of feverfew, Culpeper says: 'Venus commands this herb, and hath commended it to succour her sisters, women, and to be a general strengthener of their wombs, and remedy such infirmities as a careless midwife hath there caused.'

Flowers which come under the rulership of Venus, according to Culpeper, are violets, damask roses and periwinkle, which according to Culpeper has aphrodisiac qualities: 'The leaves eaten together by man and wife, causeth love between them'. The cowslip, foxglove, which Culpeper describes as 'being of a gentle cleansing nature, and withal very friendly to nature', and golden rod are also ruled by Venus. Culpeper considered golden rod a diuretic; as it is today. Of wild tansy or silver weed, he says: 'Now Dame Venus have fitted women with two herbs of one name, one to help conception, the other to maintain beauty, and what more can be expected of her? What now remains for you but to love your husbands, and not to be wanting to your poor neighbours?'

Mars (rules Aries and co-rules Scorpio)

Mars signifies anything that is hot, sharp, fiery, energetic or courageous. Named after the ancient god of war, it is the planet concerned with fighting and battles. Soldiers, firemen and people who use cutting equipment in their work (such as surgeons) are ruled by Mars. In an individual horoscope, the position and aspects of Mars show how assertive that person is. In the body, Mars rules the muscles, body heat and the sex functions. The quality of Mars is said to be hot and dry, and the herbs, fruits and vegetables placed under Mars are the ones which have this quality. The list includes the hot spices, such as mustard, ginger and chilli, and also horseradish, ginger, garlic and peppercorns. Onions, leeks, radishes, rocket, hops and nettles also come under Mars, as do basil, and chives, which Culpeper describes as 'hot and dry ... and so under the dominion of Mars'. Rhubarb also comes under Mars, as do nasturtiums, daffodils, toadflax, gentians, windflowers, hawthorn and broom.

Jupiter (rules Sagittarius and co-rules Pisces)

In the solar system, Jupiter is the largest of the planets, and its principle in the horoscope is of generosity, prosperity, expansion and widening of horizons. This applies both literally and metaphorically. Jupiter is the planet of long journeys and foreign countries; it is also the planet which shows the development of the mind over and above normal schooling, and it signifies interests and activities which broaden ideas and experience. It is the planet of philosophy, publishing, law and religion, and also the planet of sport, including horse racing. In the body, Jupiter rules the blood, the liver and the gall, and is linked to nutrition.

Jupiter's quality is said to be hot and moist, and the foods which come under it include asparagus, chestnuts, pinenuts, bilberries and maple syrup. Also white beetroot, which according to Culpeper 'is of a cleansing, digesting quality … good for the headache and swimmings therein, and turnings of the brain'. He adds dandelion, 'of an opening and cleansing quality', and samphire, still to be found in coastal areas, and of which he says: 'It is an herb of Jupiter, and was in former times wont to be used more than now it is; the more is the pity. It is well known almost to every body, that ill digestions and obstructions are the cause of most diseases which the frail nature of man is subject to: both which might be remedied by the frequent use of this herb… It is a safe herb, very pleasant both to taste and stomach.'

Red roses belong to Jupiter, as do purple-flowered borage, sage ('Jupiter claims this herb and bids me tell you it is good for the liver, and to breed blood'), chervil which 'doth moderately warm the stomach', and sweet cicely. Of balm, Culpeper says: 'Let a syrup be made of the juice of it and sugar be kept in every gentlewoman's house to relieve the weak stomachs and sick bodies of their poor and sickly neighbours.'

Saturn (rules Capricorn and co-rules Aquarius)

Saturn symbolizes the heavy, the restrictive, the limiting. Just as in its physical form Saturn is contained within rings, so in astrology Saturn correlates with boundaries. In the body, Saturn rules the skeleton and the skin, the formation of stones; in the world it shows organization, planning, hard work, rules and regulations, responsibilities and duties. Saturn is the planet of time and time-keeping. Clocks and watches are ruled by it. It governs tradition and old age; also the practical and the down-to-earth. It shows the land, mining, building, stone and leather, and jobs connected with these.

Mediaeval astrologers such as Culpeper used to refer to Saturn in rather gloomy terms. It was known as 'the greater malefic'; Mars being 'the lesser malefic'. Saturn was thought to show all kinds of misfortune. Modern astrologers, however, do not take this view. Events and circumstances which bring the need for self-discipline, planning and hard work may certainly feel uncomfortable at the time, but they bring the qualities which lead to success in the end. I personally regard Saturn as a most helpful planet. I will never forget working on a horoscope which showed an excellent mind, but Saturn's influence, because of its position in the horoscope, was the weakest I have ever seen. The person concerned had gained several brilliant degrees but had never been able to hold down a job for more than six months, and was more or less a scholarly recluse. The practicality and self-discipline which Saturn brings are essential in realizing the full potential of the rest of the horoscope. I would far rather see a strong Saturn in a horoscope than a strong Jupiter!

The quality of Saturn is cold and dry. Under his rulership are red beetroot, quince and comfrey, 'cold, dry and earthy in quality'. The medlar, according to

Culpeper, 'is old Saturn's and sure a better medicine he hardly hath to strengthen the retentive facility'. Also barley, which Culpeper describes as 'a notable plant of Saturn; if you view diligently the effects by sympathy and antipathy, you may easily perceive a reason of them; as also why barley-bread is so unwholesome for melancholic people.' Culpeper put mushrooms under the rulership of Saturn and did not think highly of them. Sloes, beech, elm, holly, ivy and all mosses come under Saturn, as do the service tree and the following flowers: shepherd's purse, amaranthus, 'an excellent qualifier of the unruly actions and passions of Venus' and heart's ease, with their little pansy faces.

THE EXTRA-SATURNIAN PLANETS

These planets, described below, were not known to the ancient astrologers and therefore are not linked by tradition with any ingredients. Since their discovery modern astrologers have, from observation and experience, developed an understanding of their effects and the aspects of life with which they correlate.

Uranus (co-rules Aquarius)

The quality of Uranus is said to be cold and dry. In the horoscope it shows change, the unexpected, the bizarre, the magnetic, the unconventional, the lightning flash, either literally or metaphorically. It shows inventors and inventions, scientists, astrologers, people with off-beat jobs or life-styles. It symbolizes electricity, radio waves, computers and electronics of all kinds. In the body it shows the nervous system, the pituitary gland and the spinal marrow. As far as foods are concerned, I think it shows unusual mixtures; surprise dishes; ingredients which produce an unexpected result or come in unexpected ways.

Neptune (co-rules Pisces)

Neptune is said to be cool and moist in quality. Astrologers know it to be the planet of enigma and mystery, of illusion and delusion. It shows spiritual ecstasy, martyrdom and sublime imagination; also loss of consciousness through anaesthesia and escape through alcohol, drugs or suicide. It is the planet of the occult and of the unconscious; of poetry, acting, and artistic expression; of the sea and of liquids such as oil and water. In the body, Neptune governs the pineal gland and paralysis.

As far as foods are concerned, fish and sea vegetables would come under the rulership of Neptune, also alcohol and other ingredients which bring altered states of consciousness.

Pluto (co-rules Scorpio)

Cold and dry in quality, Pluto is the planet of transformation. Its effect in the horoscope is to lead us on from one life-experience to another. Thus Pluto shows power play and manipulation, birth, death and committed relationships; it also shows the need to let go of old conditions to make way for the new. Sometimes this happens through a gradual build-up of circumstances which eventually lead to a crisis point, a dissolution of the old and a fresh start. In the world, Pluto correlates with mining, night-time and the ocean depths.

ASTROLOGY, FOOD AND HEALTH

Culpeper used his knowledge of astrology and of herbs to treat the sick. In doing so, he would either use a remedy from a plant which was similar in nature to the organ or disease concerned, on the basis of 'like taketh away like', or he would use one of the opposite quality. So if it was a heart problem, for instance, he might prescribe a herb of the Sun, which rules the heart. Alternatively, he might prescribe a substance of an opposite type, belonging to Saturn, to cure by antipathy.

Culpeper explains how this use of opposites works, when describing the effect of nettles which he places under Mars because of their hot, dry nature: 'You know Mars is hot and dry and you know well that winter is cold and moist; then you may know as well the reason why nettle tops eaten in the spring consumeth the phlegmatic superfluities in the body of man, that the coldness and moistness of winter hath left behind.'

Culpeper also further clarifies the way he uses the antipathy between planets to treat disease in this description of how he sees the nature of Mars and Venus: 'The greatest antipathy between the planets is between Mars and Venus; one is hot, the other cold; one is diurnal, the other nocturnal; one dry, the other moist; their houses are opposite, one masculine, the other feminine; one public, the other private; one is valiant, the other effeminate; one loves the light, the other hates it; one loves the fields, the other sheets; then the throat is under Venus, the quinsy lies in the throat, and is an inflammation there; Venus rules the throat, it being under Taurus, her sign. Mars eradicates all diseases in the throat by his herbs, of which wormwood is one, and sends them to Egypt on an errand never to return more, this is done by antipathy.' My own experience of writing this book has shown me how often people seemed to prefer ingredients traditionally associated with their opposite sign, fiery Ariens liking mild dishes, for example, and gentle Cancerians hot, spicy flavourings.

I have included Culpeper's comments out of interest; they, and my own comments on herbs and remedies, are not intended to be taken as suggestions for treatment. My aim has been to show how the qualities of the planets, as described, can be traced through all aspects of life, from the physical form of the planet down to fruits, vegetables and herbs. I have sought to give an understanding of the character of the signs of the Zodiac, particularly their culinary likes and dislikes, and how to please them.

ROSE ELLIOT

ARIES

Aries – the 'speedy eater' – is a Fire sign of Cardinal quality, ruled by Mars and symbolized by the ram. It is also the first sign of the Zodiac, and has in its nature all the thrusting energy of beginnings, springtime and new life. People born under this sign are vigorous, outgoing, brave and enthusiastic. They love a challenge and are great initiators of schemes and projects. Tremendously hard-working, they are also adventurous and pioneering. This is the sign of the knight, the crusader, the explorer and adventurer, and Ariens are never so happy as when they are fighting for a cause, particularly an apparently lost one.

The Fire element is evident in the warmth of the sign. Aries is the most ardent of the signs, but, as in the leaping flame, passion is seldom sustained for long. An Arien is inspired by the mood or enthusiasm of the moment. No one can inspire and motivate others like an Arien can and their enthusiasm is truly infectious. They are brilliant at beginning projects and enterprises but not so good at sustaining or finishing them. For this they need the support and backing of more practical and methodical signs such as Taurus or good organizers and delegators like Leo.

Frank and Open

Aries is an impulsive sign. People born under it do not think twice – or even once – before leaping. They therefore make mistakes and come up against red tape and authority, but for decisiveness and courage, no sign can touch them. They are also open, frank and straightforward in the way they talk. You know with an Arien that you are getting the truth as they see it and they are not going to say something different when your back is turned. They are courageous in telling you what they really think but sensitivity is not one of their strong points.

Patience, tact, and subtlety are certainly not the forte of Ariens. They are very impatient and like to go straight to their goal without any political manoeuvring. They may seem very pushy, selfish and self-centred at times and there is certainly an element of 'me first' about the typical Arien. However, they are so warmhearted and uncomplicated that it is difficult not to like them and let them get away with it.

All the Fire signs – Aries, Leo and Sagittarius – are leaders in their way. Leo leads from on high, the established king and ruler, organizing and delegating. Sagittarius leads by wisdom and teaching, but Aries leads from the front, in the heat of the battle where the action is, the true warrior-prince.

Ardent and Impatient

In relationships, Ariens are direct, ardent and impatient. Some of the more sensitive signs may find them bossy and overpowering; they can be selfish and they do like to be in control. They are also highly independent, but they make loyal friends and will rise instantly to the defence of a loved one.

Ariens enjoy an active life-style and always have many interests and outlets for their energy. At their best when rising to a challenge, they need to watch a tendency to drive themselves (and others) too hard or to cram their life too full. It might be helpful for them to consider why they have to create so much activity in their lives; it may be because deep down they fear inactivity and being dependent on other people. If they can recognize and accept that they have these fears and then let them exist without trying to repress them, the tension will subside and the pace will ease to a less frantic level!

Musical Gifts

Some form of sport or active exercise is important for Aries. Strangely, for such a straightforward sign, Aries can give marked musical gifts; the sign certainly gives the energy and alertness needed to play a musical instrument.

In their careers, Ariens are happiest when they have plenty of scope for using their initiative. They are born entrepreneurs or freelancers, good at running their own businesses. They can turn their hand to many jobs, and the greater the challenge, the better. They like work which brings quick results and has flexible hours, although they will work all hours to achieve a goal. Ariens are particularly good at jobs which use their gift for getting across ideas and inspiring others: teaching, selling, or work in advertising or public relations are some examples.

Foods for Ariens

Like those born under the other Fire signs, Leo and Sagittarius, Ariens are inclined to look upon food as fuel. They generally have healthy appetites and though their metabolism is good they may put on weight because they eat quickly, impatiently and heartily – and they love snacks! Fast food was made for Ariens because of its speed and filling quality, although it is not the healthiest way of eating and can lead to too high a fat intake, excess calories and obesity.

If they do put on weight, Ariens like to lose it quickly on a fast diet with dramatic results. They do not mind starving themselves temporarily or taking strange combinations of food for a short time if the weight loss is worthwhile and rapid.

Ariens love filling, tasty meals. They are particularly fond of cheese and dishes which include this such as deep-dish pizza, stuffed pancakes with a cheesy topping, ploughman's lunch and cheese fondue. They enjoy pasta because it can be prepared so speedily and is also filling, and they are fond of rice dishes.

Meals on the Move

Any dish which can be prepared quickly and eaten on the move appeals to an Arien: dips with crudités, meal-in-a-glass mixtures which they can whizz up in a few seconds and drink as they go out of the door; cheese and fruit, yogurt, nuts and raisins, cheese sandwiches – all 'fast foods' to suit the Arien pace, but of a more healthy variety.

Foods which are ruled by Mars and thus belong to Aries are all hot spices, including mustard, chilli and horseradish, and hot vegetables such as onions, garlic, leeks and watercress. Nettles and rhubarb belong to Aries, as do chives and basil. However, although most of the Ariens I know like well-flavoured food and delicate spices, they dislike very hot spices. They are instead drawn to the soothing foods and flavours of the opposite planet, Venus, and the cooling ingredients of Saturn, perhaps instinctively seeking balance. From Venus, thyme is particularly good, as are elderberries, to soothe fevers; also feverfew, for migraine. From Saturn, barley, perhaps made into lemon barley water, has a tranquillizing effect.

Entertaining, Arien-style

The thing about having a meal with an Arien is that they are not pretentious. They don't consider themselves to be particularly good cooks and yet they always, in my experience, seem to produce wonderful, tasty food with the maximum speed and the minimum of fuss. They are well-organized in a slightly scatty, fast-moving way. At the end of a demanding, action-packed day they are capable of fitting in a large amount of cooking while remaining bright, lively and as much fun as ever when

Deliciously rich and sticky: Caramel Squares, an
ideal gift for an Arien friend (page 29)

their guests arrive. They like entertaining buffet-style with a selection of hot and cold dishes. This informal, almost impromptu kind of hospitality suits the Arien temperament well: there can be a mixture of dishes which can be quickly prepared and laid out on the table, so the meal need not take too much advance planning.

Only the other day I went to a supper party given by one of my favourite Arien friends. She is one of the busiest people I know, with three children and a demanding career. The food, which was laid out in a simple, straightforward way, was excellent and included the delectable spiced chick pea dish which I have endeavoured to recreate. I have also had many meals with another very dear Arien friend. They have always been tasty and delicious, despite being made on the wing, as she too, is always busy. I have shared some particularly good meals of pasta and stuffed pancakes

with her, had a wonderful rice salad containing chopped apple, banana, raisins and onion with a hint of curry, and some indulgent but very easy-to-make puddings. The almost instant ice cream is her recipe and is always a winner. My sister, too, is an Arien and has the same gift for producing excellent fuss-free, unpretentious food in a hectic life. (Does anyone know an Arien who isn't busy?) Her favourite dish is Cheese Fondue, which she makes to perfection. How appropriate this dish is for fiery Aries. Ariens love foods which can be cooked rapidly at the table, before their eyes, and are often great flambéers and barbecuers – styles of cooking which are absolutely right for a Fire sign.

Ariens and Health

Aries gives abundant vitality and, like all the Fire signs, excellent recuperative powers. The main problems stem from the impulsive way in which Ariens rush around. This tends to make them rather accident-prone. They also work themselves hard and do not look after themselves as well as they might. A bit more care and nurture would actually result in improved performance. It is no use telling Ariens that they should have regular, nourishing meals and eight hours' sleep a night. With their fast-moving, erratic life-style they would find this an impossible regime. However, a stock of healthy fast-food snacks and a daily multi-vitamin tablet, plus making time for regular exercise, would be practical measures any Arien could take with advantage health-wise.

Keep Going

If they do get ill, Ariens hate to give in, and have to be practically immobilized before they will rest. Like the other Fire signs, they tend to burn off disease with a fever.

The parts of the body ruled by Aries and thus particularly susceptible to illness and accident are the head, neck and face. Migraine is a particularly Arien complaint and so is neuralgia.

Clockwise from top: Rosemary Kebabs with Herb Rice; Spiced Chick Peas; Tomato and Mozzarella Salad (page 26)

ROSEMARY KEBABS WITH HERB RICE

Rosemary, according to Culpeper, is 'under the celestial Ram. By the warm and comforting heat thereof it helpeth all cold diseases, both of the head, stomach, liver and belly.' Here tasty vegetables are threaded on to rosemary stems, to absorb a hint of the herb's flavour.

Serves 4
8 woody rosemary stems
16 pearl onions, skinned
2 medium red peppers, de-seeded and cut into
2.5 cm/1 inch squares
16 cherry tomatoes, washed, stems removed
2 tablespoons oil
salt and freshly ground black pepper
For the rice
25 g/1 oz butter
1 tablespoon olive oil
1 onion, finely chopped
225 g/8 oz brown rice, or 175 g/6 oz brown rice and
50 g/2 oz wild rice
½ teaspoon salt
600 ml/1 pint water
2 heaped tablespoons chopped fresh parsley
50 g/2 oz pinenuts or toasted flaked almonds

First prepare the rice. Melt the butter in the oil in a heavy-bottomed saucepan and fry the onion for about 5 minutes, until it is beginning to soften. Add the rice and wild rice if used, and stir well. Add the salt and water. Bring to the boil, then cover, turn the heat right down, and leave for 40 to 45 minutes until the rice is tender. Stir gently and add the parsley, nuts, and season.

Meanwhile, strip the lower leaves off the rosemary stems, leaving a sprig at the top. Blanch the onions by cooking them in boiling water for about 2 minutes; drain well. Thread the peppers, tomatoes and onions on to the stems, brush with oil and season.

About 15 minutes before serving, preheat the grill to high. Place the kebabs under the grill, keeping the leaves away from the heat. Grill for about 10 minutes, turning from time to time, until the vegetables are tender and lightly browned. Spread the rice out on a large warm dish and arrange the kebabs on top.

SPICED CHICK PEAS

The spicing in this dish is gentle, and the cream adds to its delicacy. Serve it as a side dish, or, with the addition of brown rice and a salad, as a main course.

Serves 4
2 tablespoons oil
1 large onion, chopped
½ teaspoon turmeric
1 tablespoons cumin seeds
2 × 425 g/14 oz cans chick peas, drained
1 × 142 ml/5 fl oz carton single cream
salt and freshly ground black pepper
paprika
For the brown rice (optional)
225 g/8 oz brown rice
600 ml/1 pint water
1 teaspoon salt

First prepare the brown rice, if serving. Put the rice in a heavy-bottomed saucepan. Add the water and salt. Bring to the boil, then cover the pan, turn the heat down as low as possible and leave to cook for 45 minutes.

Meanwhile heat the oil in a medium saucepan and fry the onion for 10 minutes, until soft but not browned. Add the turmeric and cumin and cook over a high heat for about 1 minute, until the cumin seeds start to pop. Reduce the heat and stir in the chick peas and cream. Cook until heated through. Season with salt and pepper, then sprinkle with paprika and serve at once. Stir the rice gently with a fork and transfer to a serving bowl.

JENNY'S CHEESE FONDUE

Although it may seem almost like a snack, cheese fondue is actually very filling. It makes an excellent quick supper for a few people, especially when served in a cosy corner of a candlelit kitchen. The communal aspect of it, with all the guests dipping happily into a shared pot, makes for an informal and intimate atmosphere that invariably adds a warm glow to the evening.

Serves 4
1 garlic clove, halved
300 ml/½ pint dry white wine or cider
400 g/14 oz Edam cheese, grated
1 tablespoon cornflour
2 tablespoons kirsch or gin (optional)
2 teaspoons lemon juice
salt and freshly ground black pepper
grated nutmeg
To serve
2 French sticks, 1 white and 1 wholemeal, cut into
bite-sized pieces and warmed in the oven

Rub the garlic around the inside of a medium saucepan or fondue dish, then discard. Place 4 tablespoons of the wine or cider in a bowl and set aside. Pour the remaining wine or cider into the saucepan and bring just to the boil. Add the cheese and stir over a gentle heat until it has melted. Add the cornflour to the reserved wine or cider. Mix well and add the kirsch or gin, if used. Pour this into the cheese mixture, stirring until the fondue is slightly thickened. Remove the saucepan from the heat and then add the lemon juice.

Season with salt, freshly ground black pepper and grated nutmeg to taste.

Put the warmed bread cubes into two baskets, mixing wholemeal and white. Place the pan of fondue in the centre of the table, and supply your guests with long forks so that they may spear pieces of bread and then dip them into the fondue.

TOMATO AND MOZZARELLA SALAD

This salad, with its garnish of the Martian herb, basil, makes a delicious first course. Use an attractive lettuce such as oakleaf or frisée.

Serves 4
4 tomatoes
100 g/4 oz Mozzarella cheese
a few lettuce leaves, torn into bite-sized pieces
fresh basil to garnish
For the dressing
2 tablespoons red wine vinegar
6 tablespoons olive oil
salt and freshly ground black pepper

Slice the tomatoes and cheese thinly and arrange on 4 individual plates, together with the lettuce. Make a dressing by mixing together the vinegar and oil in a screw-top jar. Add salt and freshly ground black pepper to taste. Close the jar tightly, shake the dressing vigorously, then spoon a little over each salad. Snip some fresh basil on to each to garnish and serve at once.

ALMOST INSTANT COFFEE AND HAZELNUT ICE CREAM

Serves 8
600 ml/1 pint whipping cream
1 × 397 g/14 oz can condensed milk
1 tablespoon good strong instant coffee
1 tablespoon boiling water
100 g/4 oz hazelnuts, skinned and chopped

In a large bowl, whip the cream until thick, then add the condensed milk and whip again. Dissolve the coffee in the boiling water and add to the cream mixture. Fold in the nuts, mix well, then pour the mixture into a polythene container and freeze until firm.

Above: Arien Flower Cake (page 28); Almost Instant Coffee and Hazelnut Ice Cream

ARIEN FLOWER CAKE

The Ariens I know love lemon sponge cake. So here is a cake specially for them, decorated with a burst of golden daffodils, their flowers. Later in the season you could use nasturtiums, also an Arien flower, or you could decorate the cake with crystallized yellow freesias. For a simple touch, use mimosa balls and diamonds of angelica.

Makes one 20 cm/8 inch ring cake
225 g/8 oz self-raising flour
2 teaspoons baking powder
225 g/8 oz caster sugar
225 g/8 oz soft butter
grated rind of 1 large lemon
4 eggs, beaten
For the filling
2 large egg yolks
50 g/2 oz caster sugar
juice and grated rind of 1 lemon
For the frosting
2 large egg whites
pinch of cream of tartar
350 g/12 oz caster sugar
bunch of wild or miniature daffodils

Preheat the oven to moderate, 160°C (325°F), Gas Mark 3. Grease a 20 cm/8 inch ring mould, and line with strips of greased greaseproof paper.

Sift the flour and baking powder into a mixing bowl, then add all the remaining ingredients and beat for 2 to 3 minutes, or until light and glossy.

Spoon the mixture into the prepared tin.

Bake for 45 to 60 minutes, until the cake has risen and springs back when touched lightly. Turn the cake out on to a wire rack to cool, carefully removing the lining paper from it.

While the cake is cooling, put all the filling ingredients into a small bowl set over a saucepan of boiling water.

Cook, stirring constantly, until the mixture thickens and coats the back of the spoon. Take the pan off the heat and allow the mixture to cool completely.

Carefully slice the cake in half horizontally. Spread the bottom half of it with the lemon filling, then replace the top half.

Make the frosting. Combine the egg whites, cream of tartar and sugar in a bowl set over a saucepan of water, making sure that the bowl does not touch the water. Whisk the mixture over the heat for about 7 minutes, or until the frosting stands in stiff peaks. Spoon and spread this all over the cake so that it covers it completely. Leave to set.

To serve, arrange the daffodils in a small bowl placed in the centre of the ring, making sure that the bowl is concealed by the flowers.

BARLEY WATER

Barley, which belongs to Saturn, traditionally has calming qualities to soothe the fiery Arien temperament. As Culpeper says, 'barley-water and other things made thereof, do give great nourishment to persons troubled with fevers, agues, and heats in the stomach'. It is still a popular drink for invalids, as well as being very refreshing on a hot summer's day.

Makes 1 litre/1¾ pints
50 g/2 oz pearl barley
1 litre/1¾ pints water
thinly peeled rind and juice of 2 medium lemons
sugar to taste

Combine the pearl barley, the measured water and the lemon rind in a large saucepan. Bring to the boil, then reduce the heat and simmer gently for 2 hours. Strain the barley water into a large jug and stir in the lemon juice and sugar to taste. Chill in the refrigerator before serving in tall tumblers.

GIFTS FOR ARIENS

Ariens like the bright, the bold, the fashionable and the fun. They prefer vivid tones, particularly flame colours – yellow, orange and red; their flowers are daffodils and nasturtiums; their birthstones are diamonds, bloodstone, amethyst and rock crystal and their metal is iron.

Flashy flamboyance *Fun presents which are also useful appeal to Ariens. They are aware of the latest styles and trends and like something which is up-to-the-minute. They don't mind bright colours and a bit of flashy flamboyance and prefer instant, disposable fashion to long-lasting classics. Something shiny, sparkling or fun to wear, such as a T-shirt with a personalized inscription might be appreciated.*

Travel and adventure *Mobility is important to Ariens, so* they would enjoy something connected with this: maps, travel books, a good compass, perhaps, or a tiny travelling alarm clock in a case, a sponge bag, a folding pocket knife or a belt-purse. Books about people who have risen to challenges and adventure will also inspire.

Efficient equipment *In the kitchen, Ariens like efficient equipment which helps them to work speedily. A very special Arien would appreciate a food processor or microwave oven, or a set of razor-sharp knives. A kebab set, barbecue or fondue set could also find favour. In the culinary line, some good quality tea, crystallized fruits or marmalade while sweet-toothed Ariens would be thrilled to receive the Caramel Squares (recipes follow).*

THREE-FRUIT MARMALADE

Makes about 2.25 kg/5 lb
1 grapefruit
3 sweet oranges
2 lemons
1.75 litres/3 pints water
1.4 kg/3 lb sugar
small knob of butter

Scrub the fruit thoroughly under warm water, then cut into quarters and put into a saucepan or pressure cooker. Add 1.2 litres/2 pints of the measured water (750 ml/1½ pints if you are using a pressure cooker). Simmer gently until the fruit is tender – about 35 to 40 minutes, or cook for 12 minutes on high pressure in a pressure cooker.

Cool, then cut up the fruit, removing the pips. Put the pulp and liquid back into the clean saucepan with the sugar and the remaining water. Heat gently without boiling until all the sugar has dissolved, then boil rapidly for about 15 minutes, or until setting point is reached (see page 141).

Stir in the butter to disperse the scum, then leave the marmalade to stand for 10 to 15 minutes. Pour into hot sterilized jars and cover. Label when cool.

CARAMEL SQUARES

Makes about 64
100 g/4 oz butter or margarine
50 g/2 oz caster sugar
175 g/6 oz plain flour
For the filling
100 g/4 oz butter or margarine
50 g/2 oz soft brown sugar
1 × 196 g/6.1 oz can condensed milk
To finish
100 g/4 oz chocolate, melted

Preheat the oven to moderate, 180°C (350°F), Gas Mark 4. Cream the fat and sugar together in a mixing bowl until light and fluffy, then stir in the flour. Turn on to a lightly floured surface and knead. Roll out to a square, press evenly into a greased shallow 23 cm/9 inch square cake tin and prick well. Bake for about 25 minutes. Cool in the tin.

Combine the filling ingredients in a saucepan and heat gently, stirring, until dissolved. Bring slowly to the boil, then cook, stirring constantly, for 5 to 7 minutes. Cool, then spread over the base and leave to set. Spread with chocolate. When set, cut into squares measuring about 2.5 cm/1 inch.

TAURUS

Taurus – the 'gourmet eater' – belongs to the element Earth, is symbolized by the bull, ruled by the planet of beauty, Venus, and is of Fixed quality.

This means that people born under the sign of Taurus are practical and down-to-earth, with plenty of common sense and sound business acumen. They like to think carefully before making a move; if they are rushed or pressurized in any way, they will dig in their toes and show why those born under this sign have the reputation for being obstinate! Once a Taurean has really decided on a course of action, he can't be budged.

People born under this sign have a calm, almost bovine quality; they do not fidget or whine or worry, like some of the more flighty signs. They take things in their stride and are quiet and stoical in the face of difficulties. Most of the time, a Taurean will be pleasant, kind, easy-going, quiet and patient. Like the bull in the field, he will get on with his own business and expect others to do the same. If, however, you annoy a Taurean, by rushing, teasing or contradicting him, he may display a rage and temper quite in keeping with his symbol. Fortunately this seldom happens.

Common Sense and Consideration
Taureans are, above all else, highly practical. If you go to a Taurean with a problem, he will first of all sit you down in a comfortable chair and make you a cup of tea, and then consider the matter thoughtfully. The solution will be based on common sense (which, along with loyalty, Taureans value above all qualities) and a realistic understanding of the situation, conditions and the likely reactions of others.

Although they like to proceed at a calm pace, and have a great need for comfort, pleasure and beauty, Taureans are capable of hard, determined work. If you are involved with Taureans in a project or enterprise, you may be sure that, as long as you pull your weight and don't antagonize them by being sloppy, lazy or disloyal, they will more than reciprocate and will be reliable, steady and a pleasure to work with.

Traditional Values
The fixed quality brings steadiness to the Taurean nature, a liking for routine, for the tried and tested and for traditional values. Taureans love the countryside.

At first glance, it may seem strange that Venus, the planet of beauty and of love, should be the Ruler of such a practical, earthy sign as Taurus. But the influence of Venus can be seen clearly in the gentle, peace-loving ways of Taureans; in their kindness and diplomacy, in their liking for comfort, pleasure and ease, and in their sensuality and love of beauty. Most Taureans are artistic and find much satisfaction through creative hobbies and crafts such as painting, dressmaking or cooking.

Foods for Taureans
The sign of Taurus is an interesting one because it is in some ways contradictory. This is as apparent in the Taurean's attitude to food as in other areas.

As you would expect from a sign whose symbol is as strong and physical an animal as the bull, Taurus indicates a vigorous appetite. Taureans like good, honest cooking and plenty of it, just like mother used to make. They are suspicious of fads and trends such as nouvelle cuisine, whose portions they regard as far too small. Good fruit cake, jacket potatoes, meat with plenty of gravy, hefty slices of home-made bread and jam, a tasty, rib-sticking casserole: these are the foods Taureans appreciate. And yet – and here we have the paradox – a Taurean is by no means an insensitive eater, unaware of the finer points of food.

Sensual Eaters

Venus brings to the Taurean character an unexpected refinement, gentleness and appreciation of beauty. It touches the decidedly physical appetites of the bull with romance, elegance and sophistication. Although Taureans have an undeniable liking for good, simple food and plenty of it, they will also notice and appreciate the aroma, flavour, colour and texture.

If you want to please a Taurean, make sure the room is fragrant, the china sparkling, the cutlery shining. The food may be simple, but it must be honest and well cooked. If you really want to spoil them, get out crisp linen, preferably in a shade of blue or soft pink, decorate the table with scented fresh flowers, light the candles and put on some soothing music. Make sure the food is well cooked and attractively served, paying attention to colour and texture, serve one or two good sound dishes, then intrigue them and delight their romantic, Venusian side with the odd frivolity, such as crisp, heart-shaped shortbreads decorated with rose-flavoured icing and crystallized rose petals, or fragrant elderflower cordial.

Shopping for Quality

Whatever they buy, whether it be sausages or shoes, herrings or a handbag, potatoes or a pullover, Taureans go for quality. They are classy shoppers, dressers and cooks; they have taste in every sense of the word and they buy the best. On the other hand, no Taurean likes waste; they will cheerfully steam an unfranked stamp off a letter for re-use, save pieces of string and make leftover crusts of bread into crumbs and store them in the freezer for future use in cooking.

Fruits and Flowers

Having Venus as their ruling planet means that there is a range of flowers, fruits, herbs and vegetables with the quality of this sign, as well as basics such as rice and wheat. The list includes mint, thyme, lovage, roses and violets for flavouring and decoration; spinach, sorrel, endive, parsnips, Jerusalem artichokes, potatoes, and all beans and peas (including the dried ones) and many luscious fruits including blackberries, cherries, strawberries, peaches, apricots, apples, pears, plums, grapes, figs, blackcurrants and elderberries. Elderflowers and daisies also come under the sign.

Foods which, by ancient astrological tradition, are said to be good for Taureans are those which belong to Mars. These supply a hot, bracing element to balance the gentleness of Venus. Included among these are mustard, horseradish – which may ease the throat and sinus troubles which sometimes affect Taureans – garlic, onion, leeks, rocket and watercress.

Taureans and Health

People born under Taurus show their love of food from an early age. Taurean babies seldom need any persuasion to finish their meals, and they will probably come back for seconds, too. This appreciation of food lasts throughout their life.

Taurus gives a good, strong physique which does not readily give way to illness. The main problem for most Taureans is that their love of good food and drink can lead to overindulgence and obesity. This may lead to problems with circulation, varicose veins, gout and kidney problems. It is interesting that one of the herbs of Venus, thus linked to both Taurus and Libra (both signs prone to kidney problems) is burdock, which is a well-known herbal cure for kidney problems. If Taureans can find a way of eating which limits the calories, they can keep in excellent health.

High-fibre, Low-fat

The best diet for a Taurean is one rich in fibre and low

Treats for food-loving Taureans: Elderflower Cordial and Rose Shortbread Hearts (page 39)

in fat. Taureans need plenty to get their teeth into. One very attractive and slim Taurean actress put it very well when she said that although she watches her weight, she likes to eat a lot – 'like a whole steamed cauliflower, with black pepper and lemon juice, for lunch'. The answer for Taureans is to fill up on steamed vegetables and huge crunchy salads, with plenty of pasta, grains, potatoes and bread – *without* too much oil or butter, and with fresh herbs, lemon juice and black pepper for flavour.

A big bowl of porridge, made with water, and just a sprinkling of sugar or raisins makes a good warming, filling breakfast for a Taurean. For lunch, a good plateful of pasta with some salad would be ideal or a large salad with plenty of fresh herbs. A jacket potato with a little soured cream and chives would also find favour or a bowl of home-made soup and some crusty bread. The evening meal should include plenty of vegetables. Of course if this way of eating becomes the norm, there's certainly room for the occasional treat.

Problem Areas

Taurus rules the throat, neck and back, and these are areas which need special care: a cold can often turn to a sore throat and Taureans need to keep their necks warm. Blackcurrants, fruit of Venus, made into a jelly or jam and taken with a little boiling water, or a wine made from elderberries, which also come under Venus, are useful cures for Taurean coughs and colds. Horseradish, borrowed from Mars, is a good cure for the sinus problems which can afflict the sign, and regular use of an iodized salt, kelp or other seaweeds will help to keep the thyroid gland – a possible sensitive spot for Taureans – healthy.

Taureans can also ensure good health by making sure they get some exercise each day, preferably in the open air. Taureans need contact with the earth and the countryside in the way that plants need water. Taureans are at their healthiest and happiest when they live in or close to the country, or have access to a garden or park where they can enjoy the open air.

Entertaining, Taurean-style

For warmth, hospitality, good food and comfort, a Taurean home takes some beating, and Taureans love to entertain. Although they love a no-expense-spared night out, most of the time they prefer to be by their own firesides. They love their friends and family to come to them. Good cooking comes naturally to Taureans; they generally have well-equipped kitchens with best-quality knives, good solid chopping boards, classic whisks, bowls and tins – no gimmicky gadgets – and heavy saucepans, perhaps made from that Venusian metal, gleaming copper. Their kitchens are havens of delicious cooking smells and they may add to their enjoyment of cooking by listening to their favourite music while they are working.

Clockwise from top: Beautiful Bread (page 38); Artichoke Risotto (page 36); Green Pea and Mint Soup

GREEN PEA AND MINT SOUP

Both green peas and mint are foods of Venus. Here they are used together to make a velvet-smooth soup.

Serves 4
25 g/1 oz butter
1 onion, chopped
225 g/8 oz diced potato
450 g/1 lb frozen peas
600 ml/1 pint water
10 sprigs of fresh mint
salt and freshly ground black pepper
caster sugar
1 × 150 ml/5 fl oz carton single cream, optional

Melt the butter in a large saucepan, add the onions and fry gently for 5 minutes. Add the potato, stir well, then cover and cook for a further 5 to 10 minutes, without browning. Stir in the peas, water and half the mint. Cover and simmer for about 15 minutes, until the potato is tender. Purée, then pass through a sieve. Season with salt, pepper and a little caster sugar. Serve hot or cold. Swirl a little cream on top of each portion if liked, and snip the rest of the mint over.

BEAN, AVOCADO AND HERB SALAD

Culpeper described beans as 'a wholesome food', and lovage as 'an herb of the Sun, under the sign of Taurus. If Saturn offend the throat ... this is your cure ...'

Serves 4
1 tablespoon red wine vinegar
3 tablespoons olive oil
salt and freshly ground black pepper
2 tablespoons chopped fresh herbs, including lovage
1 × 245 g/15 oz can cannellini beans, drained
1 ripe avocado

Combine the vinegar and olive oil in a salad bowl. Add salt and pepper with the fresh herbs and mix well to make a dressing. Add the drained cannellini beans, and mix again, gently. The salad may be left at this point for several hours for the flavours to blend thoroughly, if convenient.

Just before serving the dish, cut the avocado in half, remove the stone and peel and dice the flesh. Add the avocado to the salad, stir gently, check the seasoning, and serve immediately.

PASTA WITH SWEET PEPPERS

This lovely mixture of colours, textures and flavours will please a pasta-loving Taurean.

Serves 4
4-6 tablespoons olive oil
2 onions, sliced
3 large red peppers, seeded and cut into matchsticks
2 garlic cloves, crushed
350 g/12 oz spiral pasta, preferably a mixture of white and green
2 tablespoons chopped fresh basil
salt and freshly ground black pepper
grated Parmesan cheese, to serve

Heat the olive oil in a frying pan and add the sliced onions and peppers. Cover the frying pan and cook over a low heat for 15 to 20 minutes, until the onions and peppers are soft and lightly browned. Add the crushed garlic cloves and continue to cook for a further 2 to 3 minutes.

Meanwhile cook the pasta in plenty of boiling water for 8 to 10 minutes, or until just tender. Drain the pasta thoroughly, then add to the pepper, onion and garlic mixture, with the chopped fresh basil and salt and freshly ground black pepper to taste. Serve immediately, with grated Parmesan cheese.

ARTICHOKE RISOTTO

The Taureans I know love rice. It is a perfect food for them, low in fat yet filling. They are also fond of artichokes, so this delicate dish combines the two. Serve this risotto with a crisp green or tomato salad to make a delicious main dish.

Serves 6
4 globe artichokes
100 g/4 oz butter
1 onion, chopped
1 whole garlic clove, peeled
2 tablespoons finely chopped fresh parsley
575 g/1¼ lb Italian arborio rice
2 litres/3½ pints boiling vegetable stock
salt and freshly ground black pepper
4-6 tablespoons grated Parmesan cheese
extra grated Parmesan cheese to serve

Cut the leaves and hairy choke from the artichokes. Slice the artichoke bases into chunks. Melt 50 g/2 oz of the butter in a large, heavy saucepan and sauté the chopped onion with the artichoke hearts and the whole garlic clove. When the onion is soft and golden, add the finely chopped fresh parsley. Cook over moderate heat for a few minutes, then discard the garlic clove and add the arborio rice.

Fry the rice for a few minutes, stirring constantly, then add 250 ml/8 fl oz of the boiling stock. Cook gently until it is absorbed. Continue to cook gently, adding 250 ml/8 fl oz of the remaining stock at a time until it has all been added, and stirring the rice gently from time to time for 20 to 30 minutes. By then the rice should be tender and all the liquid absorbed.

Season the risotto with salt and pepper, stir in the remaining butter and the Parmesan cheese, and leave the risotto over a low heat for a few minutes before serving. Serve this dish with plenty of extra grated Parmesan cheese, handed separately.

BLACKBERRY AND APPLE PIE

This pie appeals to Taureans for a number of reasons: they love an afternoon in the country picking the blackberries, and the fact that these are free pleases their sense of economy; they also love a good wholesome, honest pie. Culpeper says that blackberries 'are a powerful remedy against the poison of the most venomous serpents'.

Serves 4-6
350 g/12 oz plain wholemeal flour
175 g/6 oz butter
3-4 tablespoons cold water
extra caster sugar
For the filling
350 g/12 oz blackberries
1.1 kg/2½ lb cooking apples, peeled, cored and sliced
175 g/6 oz caster sugar
40 g/1½ oz cornflour
milk

Preheat the oven to moderately hot, 200°C (400°F), Gas Mark 6. Prepare the filling: combine the blackberries and apples in a bowl, sprinkle with the caster sugar and cornflour, mix gently and set aside.

Put the flour into a mixing bowl. Rub in the butter with your fingertips until the mixture resembles fine breadcrumbs, then add the cold water and press the mixture together to form a dough. Divide the pastry into two and roll out one half to line a 20 to 23 cm/8 to 9 inch pie dish. Pile the blackberry mixture into the pie dish, heaping it up, then roll out the remaining pastry to form a crust. Press the edges together, trim them and decorate the top with the pastry trimmings. Brush the top of the pie with milk and sprinkle it as evenly as possible with extra caster sugar.

Bake the pie in the oven for 50 to 60 minutes, until the top is crisp and golden. Serve this pie hot or warm, with cream or custard.

Above: Blackberry and Apple Pie; below: Cut-and-Come-Again Cherry Cake (page 38)

BEAUTIFUL BREAD

Taureans love to sink their teeth into a hunk of good bread, and nothing delights them more than walking into a home filled with its warm aroma. Here is an easy recipe that is sure to please.

Makes two 1 kg/2 lb loaves
50 g/2 oz butter, plus 1 tablespoon
50 g/2 oz fresh yeast or 2 tablespoons dried yeast
800 ml/1⅓ pints warm water
2 tablespoons granulated sugar
2 × 25 mg vitamin C tablets, crushed
750 g/1½ lb strong plain white flour
750 g/1½ lb wholemeal flour
4 teaspoons salt
To glaze
beaten egg or milk

Using 1 tablespoon of the butter, grease two 1 kg/2 lb loaf tins. If fresh yeast is used, crumble it into a bowl, then gradually add the measured water, mixing until blended. Stir in the sugar and vitamin C. For dried yeast, pour the water into a bowl or jug, sprinkle the yeast on top and stir in the sugar. Leave in a warm place for 10 minutes until frothy, then add the crushed vitamin C tablets.

Combine the flours in a mixing bowl. Add the salt and rub in the butter, then make a well in the centre and stir in the yeast mixture. Mix to a dough with your hands. Turn the dough out on to a clean surface and knead for about 5 minutes, or until it feels smooth and silky.

Divide the dough into two equal pieces and form each into a rectangle, the same width as the long sides of the tin. Roll each rectangle up loosely and drop it into the tin, with the fold underneath. Push the corners down well with your fingers so that the centre of the dough forms a dome shape. Cover with greased polythene (a clean supermarket carrier bag is ideal) and leave in a warm place until doubled in height.

Preheat the oven to hot, 220°C (425°F), Gas Mark 7. Brush the loaves with beaten egg or milk then bake for 15 to 20 minutes. Cool on a wire rack.

CUT-AND-COME-AGAIN CHERRY CAKE

Culpeper describes cherries, one of the fruits of Taurus, as being 'cooling in hot diseases and welcome to the stomach'. Here they are combined with dried fruits to make a generous but not-too-rich fruit cake.

Makes one 20 cm/8 inch square cake
500 g/1 lb plain wholemeal flour
1½ teaspoons mixed spice
grated rind of 1 well-scrubbed orange
grated rind of 1 well-scrubbed lemon
225 g/8 oz soft brown sugar
350 g/12 oz mixed dried fruit
225 g/8 oz glacé cherries
40 g/1½ oz ground almonds
175 ml/6 fl oz sunflower oil
300 ml/½ pint milk
1 teaspoon bicarbonate of soda
2½ tablespoons vinegar
25 g/1 oz flaked almonds

Preheat the oven to cool, 150°C (300°F), Gas Mark 2. Grease and line a 20 cm/8 inch square cake tin.

Sift the wholemeal flour and spice into a mixing bowl, tipping in any bran left in the sieve. Add the orange and lemon rinds, the sugar, dried fruit, cherries and ground almonds. Mix, then add the oil and milk, and stir well.

Dissolve the bicarbonate of soda in the vinegar in a cup. Stir quickly into the mixture. Spoon the mixture into the tin, level it, then scatter with the almonds.

Bake for about 2 hours, or until a skewer inserted into the centre of the cake comes out clean. Turn out of the tin, strip off the lining paper and cool on a wire rack.

GIFTS FOR TAUREANS

Taureans appreciate the well-made, traditional and practical. They value sensual materials like velvet and natural substances like wood, leather and cotton. Soft, pastel colours are theirs, particularly gentian blue and spring green. Their flowers are violets, periwinkles, cowslips, foxgloves and damask roses; their gems are lapis lazuli, coral, emeralds, moss agate and sapphire; their metal is copper.

Pet likes Taureans adore their pets, so a bowl, edible delicacy or toy for their pampered dog, cat or other animal would be welcome.

Garden and home Many Taureans enjoy growing their own produce, so would value gardening gloves, seeds or a beautiful book on gardening – but make sure these gifts are of the best quality. The same applies to any kitchen equipment you might give. They are keen cooks and would appreciate any interesting aid or ingredient. If you are giving them equipment, make sure it is utterly practical, of traditional design and beautifully made, like a classic Sabatier knife.

Laughter lines Taureans have no time for gimmicky new-fangled gadgets. They do have a curiously basic sense of humour, though, and often appreciate something which tickles this. One Taurean friend of mine was delighted to receive a wooden egg rack. The rack consists of a tier of shallow wooden cups painted with monks' faces. When the eggs are inserted they form the bald heads above. He still smiles every time he refills it.

ROSE SHORTBREAD HEARTS

Makes about 15
100 g/4 oz butter
50 g/2 oz caster sugar
100 g/4 oz plain flour
50 g/2 oz ground rice
For the icing and decoration
175 g/6 oz icing sugar
2 tablespoons triple-distilled rosewater
few drops of red vegetable colouring
crystallized rose petals

Preheat the oven to moderate 180°C (350°F), Gas Mark 4. In a mixing bowl, cream the butter and sugar until light, then blend in the flour and ground rice. Roll the dough out on a lightly floured board to a thickness of 5 mm/¼ inch. Cut into heart shapes and place on a baking sheet. Bake for about 25 minutes, until golden brown all over and deeper brown at the edges. Cool slightly, then transfer to a wire rack.

To make the icing, sift the icing sugar into a bowl and add enough of the rosewater to make a spreading consistency. Tint pale pink. Spread the icing on top of the bicsuits and decorate with crystallized rose petals. Leave to set.

ELDERFLOWER CORDIAL

This simple and excellent recipe comes from *Hedgerow Cookery* by Rosamond Richardson, published by Penguin. Be sure to gather elderflowers which have not been polluted by car exhaust fumes.

Makes about 2.2 litres (4 pints)
20 heads of elderflowers
1.5 kg/3½ lb sugar
1.75 litres/3 pints boiled water, cooled
50 g/2 oz tartaric acid
2 lemons, sliced

Combine all the ingredients in a large saucepan and stir periodically for 24 hours. Strain and bottle. Dilute to taste with water or soda water. It is ready to drink immediately, but will keep for several months.

Summer Sorbet Freeze 600 ml/1 pint of the undiluted cordial until icy, then put into a bowl with 1 egg white and beat thoroughly until light. Freeze again until firm. Serve with a little undiluted cordial poured over each portion and decorate with fresh elderflowers if available.

GEMINI

Gemini – the 'restless eater' – is symbolized by the twins and belongs to the Air element. It is of Mutable quality, and is ruled by the planet Mercury. The essence of the sign is communication, as indeed it is with the other Air signs, Libra and Aquarius, which have a natural rapport with Gemini. In Gemini, however, this natural trait is strengthened by the influence of the ruling planet, Mercury. Like the ancient messenger of the Gods after whom it is named, Mercury brings the quality of communication and an interest in all things mental, thus reinforcing these qualities and making Gemini perhaps the most naturally clever of all the signs. There's a mental (and often physical) speed, agility and lightness which no other sign can match.

The desire to gather and to pass on information is at the heart of the Geminian nature. Someone born under this sign is always looking for new facts, new information, fresh ideas and places to explore. As one friend said of his Geminian wife: 'She will read *anything*, even the cereal packets at breakfast if the newspaper hasn't arrived.' The lively, agile Geminian mind quickly grasps a subject or sums up a situation. Their powers of observation are acute and their comments are equally sharp and to the point.

Journalists and Writers

Geminians do not, however, like delving too deeply into a subject; their strength lies in their ability to skim the surface, gather the important facts, and then pass them on to others. Many journalists, writers and commentators are born under Gemini or have the sign strongly emphasized in their horoscope. Agents, solicitors, couriers and people concerned with communications generally, such as translators, telephone operators, chauffeurs, drivers of public transport, postal workers, are all represented by Gemini. Teachers and lecturers also often have a Geminian influence in their horoscopes.

The airy element gives Geminians a need for freedom and this is accentuated by the Mutable quality. The Mutable signs – Gemini, Virgo, Sagittarius and Pisces – all have a restless quality about them. They like change and variety, can't bear being cooped up, find it difficult to finish things. They are always ready – indeed, eager – to try something new and get bored easily. Geminians find it very difficult to fit into a routine – they are far too interested in the mood of the moment – and they don't like to settle in one job for long. As they pick up skills quickly, they succeed in many different tasks.

Keen Travellers

Geminians can be scatty and forgetful, but this is only because their bright minds are darting around all over the place. They love to discover fresh interests and information, to travel and find new places, people and customs. With their sharp ear and quick brain they pick up a language quickly – or enough to communicate sufficiently – and they are also, often, excellent mimics. They love to impart information and can be excellent conversationalists.

Geminians are masters at doing two or more things at once and frequently have several projects running simultaneously – but they are not so good at seeing things through and are inclined to lose interest.

Mood Changes

The duality of the Geminian temperament is shown by their symbol, the twins. Because of the will-o'-the-wisp quality of the sign, Geminians seem to change from moment to moment like ripples of air. They can be bright and happy one moment, tired and listless the next, but these moods are generally fleeting.

Geminians are free-spirited and love to travel. You can often spot a Geminian by their constant hand gestures and inability to stop moving.

Foods for Geminians

Geminians are so interested in what is going on around them that many don't have much time for food. Geminians who are interested in food will have ideas to do with the new recipe they have invented or how to get to the latest restaurant they've discovered.

All Geminians enjoy food they can nibble. They like savoury biscuits and sandwiches, particularly toasted ones, and I don't know a Geminian who does not love avocado, especially in guacamole. Asparagus is also popular with Geminians, as is pasta, which they like cooking because of its speed.

Foreign Foods

A Geminian will enjoy a dish or a flavour for a time, then tire of it or move on to something new. They particularly enjoy tasting foreign dishes and relish being the first to introduce these to their friends. They may try different forms of eating such as vegetarianism or macrobiotic eating for a while, but generally these phases do not last. They love instant foods which save time and trouble, such as omelettes, pasta or toast. Geminians do not like to spend too much time on anything and this includes food preparation.

Routine food shopping in large supermarkets does not appeal to Geminians. They prefer the fun and variety of a street market or the convenience of a late-night corner shop. Foodie Geminians love discovering new sources of authentic ingredients.

Natural Liveliness

All the ingredients listed under Mercury belong to Gemini and have an affinity with the sign. These include carrots, celery and fennel; also parsley, marjoram, summer and winter savory, dill and caraway. Hazelnuts, mulberries and lavender are also ideal. These ingredients are, according to Culpeper, of a mercurial nature and will enhance the natural liveliness of the sign. Geminians, who tend to be hyperactive, bursting with brittle energy, need foods of an opposite nature to counteract this. Rice, which Culpeper didn't classify, but which I put under the joint rulership of Venus and the Moon, is a particularly good food for Geminians, being a grain which calms and restores balance. Yogurt too, with its calcium and B vitamins to soothe the nervous system, is another excellent Geminian food, especially with some wheatgerm and sunflower seeds stirred in.

Entertaining, Geminian-style

Geminians, like all the air signs, are extremely adaptable. They thrive on company, conversation, ideas and activity and love to get out and about.

When entertaining, Geminians are inclined to be moved by the moment. They are not ones to spend days planning an elaborate party or dinner, poring over cookery books to choose the perfect menu and taking time to find the right ingredients. They prefer to invite friends by a last-minute phone call, or throw an impromptu supper by dint of some clever shopping at the 24-hour deli they've just discovered and some ingenuity with storecupboard ingredients. Despite this lack of planning, being entertained by a Geminian can be great fun.

Element of surprise

An element of surprise will often be present in their dinner parties, so if you are invited to dine with a Geminian, be prepared for the unexpected. Each course served in a different room, for instance, or a theme meal, perhaps a medieval feast. The novel they have just been

Fast food for the busy Geminian: Club Sandwich
(page 48)

reading may inspire a literary dinner or they may choose foods which echo the same colour from starter to petits fours.

Geminians also love eating out, particularly if they can introduce others to an exciting new restaurant. They enjoy moving from one restaurant to another, perhaps starting with drinks and nibbles at a little *tapas* bar they have discovered, moving on to a trendy restaurant for the main course, then finding a third venue for dessert, coffee and dancing.

Geminians and Health

Those born under Gemini generally have light, wiry bodies. They are highly strung and are inclined to make many quick movements. It is essentially a slim, graceful sign, and many Geminians have a naturally efficient metabolism. This, together with their tendency to forget about food, can result in a very slender build. Many Geminians lose weight during times of nervous stress, although there are some who do put on weight, particularly as they get older. Eating may, for some Geminians, become a way of easing their extreme nervous tension. When under stress, they may turn to food as a way of comforting and distracting themselves, rather than to appease genuine hunger.

The secret of slimming, for these Geminians, is to follow a simple diet which does not allow cheating through being inventive! Counting calories, allowing 1,000 a day, is as good as any and well within the scope of the clever Geminian brain. It is helpful for them to work out a week's menu in advance, including foods which are rich in B vitamins, such as yogurt, wheatgerm, brown rice and wholemeal bread, and some treats to prevent boredom. This way, they won't be tempted to nibble or, for convenience' sake, eat the nearest thing at hand, because they will already have planned and bought the ingredients for the next meal.

Respiratory Problems

Other parts of the body which come under Gemini are the nervous system and all the tubes in the body such as the windpipe, oesophagus, bronchial and fallopian tubes, and the lungs and respiratory system. The shoulders, arms and hands are also indicated. These can all be vulnerable for Geminians and they need to take care; they may be susceptible to asthma, bronchitis, hayfever and respiratory problems.

In addition, Gemini's rulership of the nervous system and the highly strung nature of the sign means that many Geminians are tense and find it difficult to sleep. The B vitamin foods are particularly good for them, especially yogurt, because of the calcium it contains.

As well as watching their diet, Geminians need to learn to relax. Setting aside an hour to unwind before bed, perhaps having a warm, soothing bath, can be beneficial. Taking up yoga, or some other relaxation technique, is also a good idea.

Left: Savoury Olive Cake; right: Penne in Cream Sauce, served with a mixed salad

GUACAMOLE

Always popular with Geminians, this dip makes a good first course or nourishing snack.

Serves 1 as a snack, 2 to 3 as a starter
1 ripe avocado
1 tablespoon lemon or fresh lime juice
½ small onion, finely chopped
1 tomato, skinned, seeded and finely chopped
1 small garlic clove, crushed
½ small green chilli, seeded and finely chopped
a few fresh coriander or parsley sprigs
salt and freshly ground black pepper
To garnish
mild paprika
1 parsley sprig

Cut the avocado in half, remove the stone and peel. Chop the flesh lightly, then place in a bowl and mash with the lemon or lime juice. Add the remaining ingredients, mixing well. Check the seasoning, then spoon into a small bowl, smooth the top and sprinkle with paprika, if wished. Garnish with a parsley sprig.

PENNE IN CREAM SAUCE

Quill-shaped pasta, *penne*, seems particularly apt for articulate Geminians, although any shape could be used for this quick and easy dish. Serve with a crisp green salad dressed with lemon juice.

Serves 4
500 g/1 lb penne
1 × 300 ml/10 fl oz carton double cream
1 garlic clove, crushed
100 g/4 oz Gorgonzola cheese
salt and freshly ground black pepper
15 g/½ oz butter

Cook the penne in a large saucepan of boiling water for about 12 minutes until just tender. Meanwhile, make the sauce. Place the cream in a small heavy-bottomed saucepan; add the garlic and Gorgonzola and heat gently, stirring occasionally, until the cheese has melted. Season and keep warm over a low heat.

When the penne are cooked, drain thoroughly and return to the still-warm pan with the butter, salt and pepper. Turn the pasta on to a large warmed serving dish, or individual plates, and pour the sauce into the centre. Serve immediately.

SAVOURY OLIVE CAKE

Serves 4
2 teaspoons butter
150 g/5 oz self-raising wholemeal flour
75 g/3 oz fresh white button mushrooms, wiped and sliced
100 g/4 oz pitted green olives, chopped
75 g/3 oz Gruyère cheese, cut into small dice
2 tablespoons olive oil
75 ml/3 fl oz white wine
2 eggs, beaten

Preheat the oven to very hot, 240°C (475°F), Gas Mark 9. Line a 450 g/1 lb loaf tin with a strip of non-stick paper to cover the base and narrow sides; grease well with the butter. Place the flour in a bowl and add the mushrooms, olives, cheese, olive oil and white wine; mix lightly, then add the eggs and mix well. Spoon the mixture into the tin and level the top. Bake for 10 minutes, then turn the oven setting down to moderately hot, 190°C (375°F), Gas Mark 5, and bake for a further 20 minutes, or until the cake is risen and golden brown, and a skewer inserted into the centre comes out clean. Slip a knife around the edges of the cake to loosen it, then turn the cake out and strip off the lining paper. Serve at once.

HERB-CRUSTED TWO-CHEESE SOUFFLÉ

Those born under Gemini, an Air sign, generally like airy foods like soufflés. Here is a delightful one, delicately flavoured with the Mercurial herb, savory. It contains extra layers of creamy Gruyère cheese, which contrasts appetizingly with the crisp crust. Serve it as a starter, or as a light main course.

Serves 4
65 g/2½ oz butter
50 g/2 oz plain flour
250 ml/8 fl oz milk
75 g/3 oz mature Cheddar cheese, grated
salt and freshly ground black pepper
25 g/1 oz fresh fine wholewheat breadcrumbs
1½ teaspoons dried winter savory
4 eggs, separated
100 g/4 oz Gruyère cheese, cut into 5 mm/¼ inch cubes

Preheat the oven to moderately hot, 190°C (375°F), Gas Mark 5. Melt 50 g/2 oz of the butter in a large saucepan and stir in the flour. Cook for 1 to 2 minutes. Gradually stir in the milk and cook, stirring until thickened. Remove from the heat, stir in the grated Cheddar and set aside to cool slightly, then season to taste.

Meanwhile, prepare the dish. Grease a 1 litre/1¾ pint soufflé dish or straight-sided casserole (or cake tin) generously with the remaining butter. Set aside 2 tablespoons of the breadcrumbs and ½ teaspoon of the savory for the topping. Mix the remaining crumbs and savory together and press the mixture into the butter to form a crisp crust for the soufflé.

Add the egg yolks to the flour mixture in the saucepan and stir well. Whisk the egg whites in a greasefree bowl until they form peaks. Stir 1 tablespoon of the beaten egg white into the cheese mixture to lighten it, then tip the rest of the egg white on top of the cheese mixture and gently fold it in.

Pour one third of the mixture into the prepared dish, then sprinkle half the cubed Gruyère cheese evenly on top. Add another third of the soufflé mixture, followed by the remaining cubed cheese and the rest of the soufflé mixture. Sprinkle the reserved breadcrumbs and savory on top, then bake for 40 minutes, until the soufflé is puffed-up and golden. Serve immediately, with French beans, baby carrots and a tomato salad.

MERINGUES

Full of air, and sandwiched in pairs – what could be more appropriate for Gemini?

Makes 6 double meringues
2 egg whites
a pinch of cream of tartar
100 g/4 oz caster sugar
2 tablespoons cocoa powder
1 × 284 ml/10 fl oz carton double cream
butter and flour to prepare baking sheet

Preheat the oven to cool, 150° (300°F), Gas Mark 2. Line a baking sheet with a piece of greaseproof paper, grease with butter or cooking oil and sprinkle with flour.

Put the egg whites into a clean, grease-free bowl with the cream of tartar and whisk until stiff and dry. You should be able to turn the bowl upside down without the egg white falling out. Whisk in half the sugar. Add the remaining sugar and whisk well. Drop tablespoons of the mixture on to the baking sheet, making 12 meringues.

Put the meringues into the oven, then reduce the temperature to very cool, 110°C (225°F), Gas Mark ¼. Bake the meringues for 1½ to 2 hours, until they have dried out. Turn the oven off and leave the meringues in the oven to cool. Remove the meringues from the baking tray with a palette knife. Combine the cocoa powder with a little cream, then gradually add the remaining cream and whip until thick. Use to sandwich the meringues together in pairs. Serve as soon as possible.

Above: Gemini Marble Cake (page 48); below: Meringues

GEMINI MARBLE CAKE

A two-tone cake for the sign of the twins...

Makes one 20 cm/8 inch round cake
350 g/12 oz plain flour
1½ teaspoons baking powder
225 g/8 oz soft butter or polyunsaturated margarine,
plus 2 teaspoons
225 g/8 oz caster sugar
4 eggs, beaten
3 tablespoons milk
1 teaspoon vanilla essence
15 g/½ oz cocoa powder
2-3 tablespoons water
For the icing and decoration
350 g/12 oz icing sugar, sifted
3-4 tablespoons water
2 teaspoons cocoa powder

Preheat the oven to moderate, 180°C (350°F), Gas Mark 4. Using 2 teaspoons of the butter or margarine, grease a 20 cm/8 inch round cake tin, and base-line with greased greaseproof paper. Sift the flour and baking powder together. Cream together the butter or margarine and the sugar until light and fluffy, then gradually add the eggs, the milk and the vanilla essence, whisking well after each addition. Gently fold in the flour and baking powder with a metal spoon. Spoon half the mixture into another bowl.

Blend the cocoa powder with the water to make a smooth runny paste. Stir this gently into half of the cake mixture. Put small spoonfuls of the two mixtures into the tin, alternating them to give an attractive marbled pattern. Smooth the top very gently. Bake in the preheated oven for 1½ hours, or until a skewer inserted in the centre comes out clean. Cool on a wire rack, then strip off the lining paper.

In a bowl, mix the icing sugar with the water to make an icing which will coat the back of a spoon thickly.

Reserve two tablespoons of the mixture; pour the rest over the top of the cake, giving the cake several sharp taps so that the icing runs smoothly all over the top and down the sides. Using a palette knife, quickly smooth the sides. Mix the rest of the icing with the cocoa powder and water. Place this in a piping bag and pipe a spiral of rings on top of the cake, then draw several 'lines' with the point of a knife from the outside to the centre of the cake to create a scalloped effect. Leave to set. Alternatively, dust with icing sugar and cocoa powder.

CLUB SANDWICH

A substantial yet filling snack for Geminians on the wing who haven't too much time to spend on such mundane activities as eating.

Serves 1
3 slices wholewheat bread, toasted
butter
a little wholegrain mustard
2 lettuce leaves
1 small tomato, sliced
a little mayonnaise, optional
1 slice cheese
1 tablespoon sweet chutney or pickle
To finish
4 stuffed olives

Spread 1 slice of toast with a little butter and mustard and arrange the lettuce leaves and tomato slices on top. Spread lightly with mayonnaise and more mustard, if liked. Butter both sides of the second slice of toast and place on top of the first layer. Top with the cheese and chutney. Spread the remaining slice of toast with butter and invert on top to complete the sandwich. Press down firmly, then cut the sandwich into quarters. Spear each quarter sandwich with a cocktail stick and decorate with a stuffed olive.

GIFTS FOR GEMINIANS

Geminians like the novel, the intellectual, the witty and stylish. They love surprises and variety. Their colours are black, white and bright, sharp yellow; their gems are topaz, beryl, aquamarine and emerald; their flowers are ferns, lilies of the valley, honeysuckle and lavender, and their metal is mercury.

Pinboards and scrapbooks *Any writing materials usually appeal to Geminis. They like pinboards or scrapbooks to display their many cuttings, magnetic clips, amusing writing paper and revolving address books.*

Making it easy *Gadgets which will help them to live their hectic life more efficiently are also very much appreciated.*

Suggestions range from a clock radio with a snooze button to an excellent corkscrew.

Busy minds *Gemini rules the hands as well as the brain, so any art or craft materials would be welcome and would help to soothe and relax the busy Geminian mind.*

Foreign flavours *In the food line, Geminians would appreciate good tea, coffee, or something stronger, perhaps Mulberry Gin (see below). Many Geminians are reluctant cooks, so might appreciate a homely present of a cake or some bread. A gift from a foreign country would be most acceptable – pistachios from Greece perhaps, extra virgin oil from Italy or wild mushrooms from a Paris market.*

ALMOND MACAROONS

Wrapped in cellophane and tied with yellow ribbon, these make a good gift for a Geminian friend.

Makes 24
100 g/4 oz ground almonds
175 g/6 oz caster sugar
2 egg whites
a few drops of real almond essence
2 tablespoons granulated sugar
12 blanched almonds, split in half
butter and flour or rice paper for preparing the baking sheets

Preheat the oven to moderate, 180°C (350°F), Gas Mark 4. Grease and flour two baking sheets, or line the baking sheets with rice paper.

Put the ground almonds and sugar into a bowl and mix together. Beat the egg whites lightly with a fork, just enough to break them up, then add gradually to the ground almond mixture, mixing gently to make a stiffish consistency. You may not need all the egg white. Flavour with a few drops of real almond essence.

Pipe or spoon the mixture on to the baking sheets, to make mounds about 1 cm/½ inch across. Sprinkle each with a little granulated sugar and press an almond half on top. Bake for about 15 minutes, until firm to the touch. Cool slightly, then remove from the baking sheet, tearing around the rice paper, if used. Cool on a wire rack.

MULBERRY GIN

Mercury's fruit, the mulberry, gives a delicate flavour to this pale pink drink. If mulberries are not available, use sloes, pricking them all over with a darning needle before placing them in the jar.

Makes 450 ml/¾ pint
225 g/8 oz mulberries
50 g/2 oz sugar
6 blanched almonds, bruised
450 ml/¾ pint gin

Put the mulberries into a 1.2 litre/2 pint jar with the sugar and the almonds and cover with the gin. Shake every few days to dissolve the sugar. Store for at least 3 months. This tastes better and better as time goes by and is excellent after a year if you can keep it that long!

CANCER

Cancer, the 'caring eater', homemaker and nurturer, is a Water sign of Cardinal quality. It is ruled by the Moon and symbolized by the crab. In common with people born under the other Water signs, Scorpio and Pisces, Cancerians are sensitive and emotional. They may deny this, because, like their symbol, the crab, they are inclined to protect their vulnerability with a shell. Cancerians do feel things keenly – the atmosphere in a room, the feelings of others, the mood of the moment. They are both imaginative and sympathetic, so if they sense someone's distress, they will immediately visualize how that person must be feeling and either help or feel torn and unhappy themselves. This can make Cancerians unduly fussy and protective – they are the natural carers of the Zodiac. The vivid imagination they share makes them inclined to envisage the worst and to worry unnecessarily, so it is helpful if they can consciously cultivate optimistic, outgoing qualities. It is a good idea for Cancerians to cultivate an empathetic approach to others, listening and reflecting sympathy without becoming caught up in any problems.

Home-loving

No Cancerian feels completely secure until he has his own home, but although they are home-lovers, they are also adaptable, and Cancerians can get on easily with many different types of people if they wish. At the same time, however, they are very private people and show their real feelings to few others. Making the effort to go outside the home may be difficult, but once they have made the effort to go out, they enjoy it. In fact, like its opposite, Capricorn, Cancer can be quite an ambitious, active sign, thanks to the influence of the Cardinal quality, and people born under it are capable, creative, goal-orientated and frequently successful once initial reserve has been overcome.

They are extremely determined and tenacious in a quiet, unobtrusive way. They may take time to make up their minds and you may think that they have given up a particular aim, but, like Scorpios, Capricornians and Taureans, Cancerians do not give up at all easily! This is neatly illustrated by their symbol, the clinging crab.

Conflicting Demands

Cancerians often feel pulled between the conflicting demands of ambition and ability on one hand and home and domestic life on the other. They need to get a balance – for they need both aspects in their life – in order to be truly happy and in harmony.

In relationships, Cancerians are kind and caring and extremely loyal, but should watch a tendency to be too possessive. They are also inclined to live in the past, making themselves unhappy with old memories instead of enjoying the present. It is important for Cancerians to guard against becoming too emotionally dependent in any relationship, or allowing others to become too dependent on them.

Cancerians tend to lack confidence in themselves and can be very self-deprecating. When they feel over-powered by more dominating, less sensitive people, they are inclined to retire into their shell. But, like the moon, which takes its light from the sun, Cancerians need others to draw them out. In the right company, when they feel comfortable and relaxed, they can reveal their true personalities and become animated, amusing, warm and fun to be with.

Collectors

Hobbies connected with the home, cooking and caring often appeal to Cancerians; they like to express their creativity artistically or through homemaking skills. Their love of the past is often reflected in an interest in history, or in collecting historical artefacts. They can be great collectors, even hoarders, unless they have one of the more uncluttered signs, such as Aquarius, emphasized in their horoscope!

Many Cancerians work in jobs connected with the home, property or domestic matters, and they are to be found in abundance in the catering and caring professions. They often have a strong business sense (and are naturally thrifty) which draws them to professions where these gifts can be used.

Foods for Cancer

Cancerians love food – almost any food, although many have a preference for creamy concoctions, both sweet and savoury. Food which reminds them of childhood is often popular; they may enjoy nursery dishes such as bread-and-butter pudding. They go for quality and tradition rather than fashionable gimmickry and are rather suspicious of the new. This is typical of the Cancerian loyalty and lack of adventurousness, although they will try foreign cuisines, and particularly like French, Indian, Japanese and Chinese food.

Cancerians enjoy all kinds of seafood. They also like mayonnaise, and dishes containing this, such as a really good home-made coleslaw. Cream, soft white cheeses, yogurt, avocado, creamy soups and dips are also favourites, as are fools. Ingredients which come under their sign and which they often enjoy are cucumbers, melons and all members of the marrow/squash family; lettuce; cabbages, cauliflowers and all other brassicas. They love the soothing, starchy quality of potatoes, particularly when mashed to a smooth cream, baked in

jackets and served with soured cream or coleslaw, or puréed and made into a warming and filling soup.

Spice Notes

When it comes to flavouring, I have noticed that many Cancerians love the hot vegetables and spices which belong to Mars. These supply a bracing quality which, according to traditional astrological law, balances the gentleness of the sign. So onions, garlic, chillis and all the warming spices often appeal and many Cancerians love Indian curries and hot South American dishes.

Cancerians are shrewd, careful shoppers. Not only have they natural thrift and business sense, but they also know exactly what to look for, particularly when buying fresh produce, and will only accept the best. Generally, they are inclined to buy more food than they need and their storecupboards are well stocked for emergencies.

Entertaining, Cancerian-style

Although Cancerians are theoretically hospitable and enjoy entertaining others, in practice a natural reserve and lack of confidence may make them hesitate to issue invitations. They are inclined to wait for others to make the first move, so that they know they won't be rejected. Sometimes, too, they are so family-orientated that either the circle is too close-knit, or they feel little need to invite others into the home. However, when you cross the threshold it is difficult not to feel comfortable in a Cancerian's home, for it is created and cared for with love and imagination.

The focus of the home is usually the kitchen. Warm and welcoming, it is likely to reflect the owner's love of cooking. It may well feel old and well used, rather than freshly renovated, since Cancerians get attached to what they know and love and sentiment matters more than slick efficiency.

Imaginative Meals

Many Cancerians are excellent cooks and enjoy using

Avocado with Green Herb Sauce (page 56), an easy Cancerian starter or snack

extremely receptive to others' moods. It is always helpful for a Cancerian to have a shower or bath after being in difficult or depressing conditions. This contact with their element helps to cleanse them physically and emotionally, as does being by the sea, a river or lake.

Cancerians do not have a great deal of vitality, although they have considerable tenacity. It is very good for them to exercise, because this helps to increase the energy-flow and make them feel more positive.

Parts of the body ruled by Cancer are the breasts and the stomach. Nerves and pent-up emotions affect their digestive systems very easily, and when under stress, Cancerians need soothing foods. Too much milk and dairy produce are not good for them, however, tending to form mucus. As a beverage, a diuretic herb tea such as golden rod (solidago) would be much better than milk and they would benefit from a soothing home-made soup such as potato and onion (recipe follows). For energy and vitality Cancerians need plenty of foods with life-force in them such as wholegrains, nuts, sprouted seeds, salads, fresh fruit and vegetables.

their culinary skills to please their loved ones. If you are invited to dine with a Cancerian, you may be sure the food will be imaginative and delicious, and that there will be plenty of it. Creamy, rich sauces often feature, and they like making (and eating) spectacular creamy desserts such as ice creams and parfaits. A truly dedicated Cancerian host or hostess will match the wines carefully to the dishes in the various courses. The only thing which Cancerians need to watch is that in their desire to make their guests feel happy and at home they do not fuss and worry too much.

Cancerians and Health

The influence of the sign's ruler, the Moon, is very evident in the rapidly changing moods of a typical Cancerian. They can appear to be in deep despair one moment and full of *joie de vivre* the next. They are also

Fluid Retention

Like the other Water signs, Cancer often gives a metabolism which inclines towards fluid retention. Reducing the intake of both salt and coffee can help here, as can the use of naturally diuretic ingredients such as bilberries and asparagus. Cancerians often have a tendency to put on weight, partly because of their love of cooking and eating and also because they often prefer being in the home rather than taking part in strenuous outdoor activities. They are inclined to eat in order to suppress feelings, often of anger, when their needs are not being met. Any Cancerian with this problem would find a book or course on assertiveness helpful.

One of the main ways in which a Cancerian can help him- or herself to excellent health is to stop worrying and take a more positive and easy-going approach to life; to watch a tendency to dwell on the past and on slights (real or imagined) and to relax and enjoy life.

Above: Potato and Onion Soup; below: Wild Mushroom Quiche

WILD MUSHROOM QUICHE

This is a perfect quiche with thin, crisp pastry and a delicious light, creamy filling.

Serves 4-6 as a main course, 6-8 as a starter
50 g/2 oz plain wholemeal flour
50 g/2 oz plain flour
pinch of salt
50 g/2 oz butter
1 egg yolk
2-3 teaspoons cold water
chopped fresh parsley, to serve
For the filling
40 g/1½ oz butter
225 g/8 oz wild mushrooms or button mushrooms,
wiped and sliced
1 small onion, sliced
1 garlic clove, crushed
3 egg yolks, lightly beaten
1 × 150 ml/5 fl oz carton single cream
4 tablespoons milk
salt and freshly ground black pepper
freshly grated nutmeg

Preheat the oven to moderately hot, 200°C (400°F), Gas Mark 6. Put a baking sheet into the centre of the oven to heat. Lightly grease a 23 cm/9 inch flan dish. Combine the flours and salt in a mixing bowl. Rub in the butter until the mixture resembles fine breadcrumbs, then add the egg yolk and enough cold water to make a smooth, pliable dough. Roll out the dough to fit the flan dish, then press it in, building the sides up above the top of the dish. Prick the dough, then bake for 20 minutes.

Meanwhile, prepare the filling. Melt half the butter in a saucepan. When it is really hot, add the mushrooms and cook quickly for about 4 minutes or until tender, stirring frequently. Remove from the heat. In another pan, melt the rest of the butter and fry the onion for about 10 minutes; add the crushed garlic. Set aside.

Remove the flan from the oven and brush the base generously with some of the egg yolk. Return to the oven for 4 to 5 minutes, until set, shiny and golden brown. Reheat the onion mixture so that it is sizzling then spread it all over the base of the flan case.

Reduce the oven temperature to moderate, 180°C (350°F), Gas Mark 4. In a bowl, combine the remaining egg yolks, cream and milk. Add a generous seasoning of salt, pepper and grated nutmeg and whisk well. Using a slotted spoon, transfer the mushrooms to the flan case and pour the egg yolk mixture on top. Bake for about 30 minutes, or until the filling is set and lightly browned. Serve hot or warm, sprinkled with parsley and accompanied by a salad or steamed vegetables.

POTATO AND ONION SOUP

This simple, warming soup is enormously soothing to the digestive system and will please any Cancerian.

Serves 4-6
2 large onions, chopped
1 large leek, roughly chopped
2 medium potatoes, cut into large pieces
900 ml/1½ pints water
25 g/1 oz butter or margarine
4-6 tablespoons single cream
salt, pepper and freshly grated nutmeg

Reserve half the chopped onion. Put the rest into a large saucepan with the leek and potatoes. Add the water. Bring to the boil, lower the heat and simmer gently for 15 to 20 minutes or until the vegetables are tender.

Meanwhile, fry the reserved onion in the butter in a frying pan for 10 to 15 minutes or until soft and golden.

Purée the potato mixture with the cream in a blender or food processor, then return to the saucepan. Add the fried onion and stir in salt, pepper and nutmeg to taste. Reheat gently without boiling and serve at once.

AVOCADO WITH GREEN HERB SAUCE

Serves 4
1 tablespoon finely chopped parsley
1 tablespoon finely chopped chives
1 tablespoon finely chopped basil
1 tablespoon finely chopped mint
300 ml/½ pint plain yogurt
4 tablespoons good quality mayonnaise
salt and freshly ground black pepper
2 ripe avocados
4 sprigs of basil or mint to garnish

First make the sauce. Either mix the finely chopped herbs with the yogurt and mayonnaise, or combine all the ingredients in a food processor or blender and whizz together. Season with salt and pepper.

Just before serving, halve, stone and skin the avocados. Pour a pool of the green herb sauce on to 4 individual serving dishes. Cut each avocado in half vertically, leaving the slices joined at the top, then fan out the slices and place on top of the sauce. Decorate with a small sprig of basil or mint and serve at once.

MIXED LEAF SALAD WITH HOT GARLIC CROUTONS

Serves 4-6
½ small red leaf lettuce and ½ small curly-leaf lettuce,
or 1 packet mixed continental lettuce
2 heads chicory
a few tender dandelion leaves (optional)
1 bunch or packet watercress
For the dressing
1 tablespoon Poupon Grey mustard
salt and pepper
1 tablespoon red wine vinegar
3 tablespoons virgin olive oil

For the garlic croûtons
vegetable oil for frying
4-6 slices of wholewheat bread, crusts removed, cut into
5 mm/¼ inch cubes
2 garlic cloves, crushed

Wash the salad leaves and shake dry. Shred whole leaves as necessary and put them into a salad bowl.

Put the mustard into a small bowl with salt, pepper and vinegar. Stir to blend, then gradually add the oil, stirring or whisking with a fork, until thick and smooth.

Just before serving, make the croûtons. Cover the base of a frying pan generously with oil and place over moderate heat. When hot, add the bread and garlic and fry, stirring, until the croûtons are golden brown all over. Drain on crumpled absorbent kitchen paper.

Give the dressing a stir, pour it over the salad and mix quickly. Add the croûtons and serve immediately.

TOASTED ALMOND ICE CREAM

Serves 8
4 eggs
225 g/8 oz caster sugar
150 ml/¼ pint water
1 × 284 ml/10 fl oz carton whipping cream
100 g/4 oz flaked almonds, toasted and cooled

Put the eggs into a bowl and whisk until frothy but not thick. Dissolve the sugar in the water in a saucepan over a gentle heat, then raise the heat and boil vigorously for 3 minutes.

Immediately pour this hot syrup over the eggs in the bowl, whisking all the time. Continue to whisk until the mixture becomes thick, then leave until cool. Whip the cream in a bowl or jug and add to the cooled egg mixture, together with the almonds. Pour into a suitable container for freezing, and freeze, uncovered, until firm. Remove from the freezer 15 minutes before serving.

Above: Toasted Almond Ice Cream; below: Claire's Cake (page 58)

CLAIRE'S CAKE

Invented by my 10-year-old Cancerian daughter, Claire, this sweet, light cake looks very pretty when decorated with either crystallized white rose petals or daisies, both Cancerian flowers. For details of how to crystallize flowers, see page 141. For a more simple effect, fill the cake with whipped cream as well as jam, and sprinkle with caster sugar.

Makes one 18 cm/7 inch round cake
100 g/4 oz self-raising flour
1 teaspoon baking powder
100 g/4 oz sugar
2 eggs
7 tablespoons sunflower oil
For the filling and topping
2-3 tablespoons warmed jam
100 g/4 oz icing sugar
1-2 tablespoons warm water
crystallized daisies or white rose petals

Preheat the oven to moderate, 160°C (325°F), Gas Mark 3. Grease two 18 cm/7 inch cake tins and line the bases with circles of greased greaseproof paper. Sift the flour, baking powder and sugar into a large mixing bowl. In another bowl, whisk the eggs and add the sunflower oil, then pour this into the flour, baking powder and sugar mixture. Beat until the mixture forms a batter.

Divide the mixture between the two prepared cake tins. Bake in the oven for 20 minutes, or until the cakes spring back when touched lightly in the centre. Carefully turn the cake layers out on to a wire rack and leave to cool.

To finish the cake, spread one layer with jam and place the other on top. Sift the icing sugar into a bowl; add enough of the warm water to make a pouring consistency, then spread the icing over the top of the cake. Finally, decorate the top with crystallized daisies or white rose petals.

POPPY SEED BAPS

Light and soft, these are topped with poppy seeds, which traditionally belong to the sign of Cancer.

Makes 8
150 ml/¼ pint milk
150 ml/¼ pint water
50 g/2 oz butter
225 g/8 oz wholemeal flour, plus extra for dusting
225 g/8 oz strong white flour
1 teaspoon salt
1 teaspoon sugar
1 × 7 g/¼ oz sachet easy-blend yeast
a little milk to glaze
1-2 tablespoons poppy seeds

In a saucepan, heat the milk, water and butter gently until the butter melts; cool to lukewarm.

Mix the flours, salt, sugar and yeast in a large bowl, then add the milk mixture and mix to a dough. Knead for 5 minutes, then transfer the dough to a lightly greased bowl. Cover with greased polythene and leave in a warm place for about 1 hour, until the dough is doubled in bulk and springs back when lightly pressed with a finger. Preheat the oven to hot, 220°C (450°F), Gas Mark 7.

Knock back the dough, then knead it again briefly. This second kneading will get rid of any air bubbles in the dough, and will ensure that it rises evenly and has a smooth texture. Divide the dough into 8 pieces, form these into smooth rounds, dust each with a little flour and place on a floured baking sheet. Brush the tops of the baps with milk and sprinkle with poppy seeds, then cover and leave in a warm place for 15 to 20 minutes, until well risen.

Bake in the oven for 15 to 20 minutes. If you want the baps to have a crisp crust, cool them on a wire rack; if you prefer them soft, wrap them in a soft cloth before leaving to cool.

GIFTS FOR CANCERIANS

Cancerians like traditional things, natural materials, objects with historical or sentimental connotations and imaginative gifts which are also practical. Their colours are sea shades: soft grey, blue, green, turquoise, all shades of blue. Their gems are emeralds, black onyx, moonstone and pearl, their flowers are moon-daisies, poppies, lilies, wallflowers and white roses; and their metal is silver.

Simply sentimental *Cancerians are sentimental and are often delighted with apparently simple gifts from children or adults dear to them. They will not only treasure the gift but will probably keep the wrapping paper and card as well.*

Classic design *Lace, silver and antiques appeal to Cancerians; they like classic design, items of historical significance and things to do with the sea, such as shells.*

Home and garden *Small gifts for the home, such as a pastel linen tablecloth, a pretty vase, silver photograph frame or some crystal candle holders, would be popular. So would almost anything for the kitchen: a traditional French ovenproof casserole dish or a bag of mixed peppercorns, mustards with different flavourings, or flavoured oils or vinegars (see below). For the garden or windowsill, a pot of herbs would always be welcome.*

FLORENTINES

Makes 12
50 g/2 oz butter
50 g/2 oz caster sugar
75 g/3 oz flaked almonds
25 g/1 oz mixed peel, chopped
50 g/2 oz cherries, roughly chopped
2 teaspoons lemon juice
100 g/4 oz plain chocolate

Melt the butter in a saucepan, then add the sugar and bring to the boil, stirring all the time. Remove from the heat and add the almonds, peel, cherries and lemon juice. Cool slightly.

Line baking sheets with non-stick baking parchment and spoon the mixture on to these, leaving plenty of space for spreading. Flatten each florentine with a fork, then bake for about 12 minutes, or until golden brown. Leave the biscuits on the baking sheets to cool for 4 to 5 minutes, or until firm enough to lift with a fish slice. Transfer to a wire rack to cool completely.

Melt the chocolate in the top of a double boiler and spread this on the flat side of each florentine. Allow to cool a little, then draw the prongs of a fork in wavy lines across the surface and leave to set completely.

FLAVOURED OILS AND VINEGARS

A few sprigs of herbs in a bottle of olive oil or wine vinegar impart a wonderful fragrance and create a delightful gift for any Cancerian who loves to cook. They make the most delicious and unusual dressing for salads, and it is almost worth cooking with a herb-flavoured oil just for the sheer pleasure of savouring the wonderful aroma wafting from the frying pan.

Put the herbs into a jar with the oil or vinegar and a pinch of salt. You can add one or two peppercorns, too, for extra zing. Shake the jar, then leave it in a sunny place for 2 weeks, shaking the jar from time to time.

At the end of this period, strain the vinegar or oil and pour it into an attractive sterilized bottle, adding a few fresh sprigs of the chosen herb if liked.

Tarragon, rosemary and thyme make delicious vinegars, as does a mixture of equal parts of mint, chives and basil. For the last-mentioned, crush the leaves lightly, put them into a jar and top up with white wine vinegar, then leave for 14 days as described above.

A delicious fruit vinegar can be made by half filling a jar with raspberries or blackberries, and topping up the jar with vinegar. Leave to stand as described, then strain and pour into a sterilized bottle.

LEO

Leo – the 'flamboyant eater' – is a Fire sign. It belongs to the Fixed group and is symbolized by the lion and ruled by the Sun. Like people born under the other Fire signs, Aries and Sagittarius, with whom Leos have natural affinity, Leos have warm, outgoing natures, and are full of ideas, courage and initiative. The Fixed quality also gives loyalty, willpower, faithfulness and determination.

It is a wholehearted sign. Leos never do anything by halves; in fact, they are inclined to overdo things. They think big. They are generous and have a sense of drama which can be observed in the way they dress, the way they live – everything about them, in fact!

Praise and Flattery

You can't give a Leo too much praise and flattery – it is music to the ears and balm to the soul. An unappreciated Leo, craving affection, is a sorry sight. They have bubbly, optimistic natures, and it takes a great deal to squash them. Equally the Leo who was constantly put down or starved of love when young may seem more reserved and less confident than is typical of the sign.

The lion, king of animals, is a very apt symbol, for this is the most regal of signs, and people born under Leo have a natural dignity which commands respect. This may be completely unconscious on the part of the Leonine individual, but others certainly feel it and instinctively respond. Many Leos behave in a lordly way, gravitating automatically to the best position or the most comfortable chair as if by right. Fortunately, they do this so openly and naturally that it is impossible to feel irritated with them for long. They expect the best, and generally get it.

Natural Leaders

Leadership comes naturally to Leos and they love being in the limelight. They can antagonize others by being too bossy and boastful and need to temper these characteristics with sensitivity and flexibility.

Leo is a playful sign and even the most serious of Leos has an almost childlike way of entering into life with enthusiasm. They are always ready for new projects or enterprises, especially if these involve organizing others. If there is an element of drama or of dressing-up involved, they are really in their element!

Spare-time activities which appeal to Leos often involve colour or music, or are creative in some way. They love music and dance and many express their creativity through these or through painting or crafts. They also have a natural rapport with children and young people.

Entrepreneurs

Any of these interests may extend to careers. Many actors, actresses, singers, dancers, pop stars and entertainers are to be found under this sign, as are entrepreneurs of all types, teachers, youth leaders and people concerned with leisure and pleasure, the travel industry, fashion and jewellery.

Foods for Leos

The Leonine ability to enjoy life extends to food, which Leos love. Most Leos have hearty appetites. Like the other Fire signs, they generally have good metabolisms which burn off the calories, especially if they are athletically inclined. Most Leos dislike too much exertion, although some sports, particularly sociable ones like tennis, can appeal. Like their symbol, the lion, they prefer relaxing and basking in the sun, although they share with their symbol the ability to be extremely energetic if they wish.

Leos like generous portions, and although they appreciate colourful, well-garnished food, they have quite simple tastes – just the best! – and don't like food which is over-sauced. They are not at all keen on the minuscule portions of *nouvelle cuisine*, regarding these as pretentious and silly. For the kings of the Zodiac, their tastes are surprisingly modest, but they do look for quality. 'Just something simple,' they will say. What a Leo means by this may be the tenderest young artichokes, spears of juicy plump asparagus with butter, a crystal bowl of fresh sweet strawberries, a glass or two of chilled vintage champagne, a few luxury hand-made chocolates ... simple food! True, they do also like peasant foods like baked potatoes and good home-made bread, often preferring these on their own, rather than mixed with other ingredients or flavourings.

Lemon and Spice

In my experience, most Leos love the clear, sharp flavouring of lemon; they also like warm spices, particularly cinnamon, and they favour dried fruits such as dates and raisins. In common with other Fire signs, they enjoy food crisp, even slightly charred, such as hard-baked water biscuits and barbecued foods. They do not care for soured dairy products such as yogurt, although they might make an exception for best quality thick creamy Greek varieties.

All the foods which traditionally come under the rulership of the Sun belong to Leo. This includes bay, rosemary, lovage and juniper for flavouring; golden saffron, most precious of the spices, for both flavouring and colouring; camomile, perhaps taken as a tea, for soothing and inducing sleep. Oranges and walnuts also belong to Leo, as do angelica and sunflowers (and sunflower seeds) and marigolds.

Shopping in Style

Although Leos love shopping for gifts, clothes and luxuries – even just window shopping when they can enjoy the colour and extravagance of the displays – they are not keen on routine food shopping. They prefer to have a standard order delivered for basics, and to telephone an order to an exclusive shop for delivery on a special occasion! If this sounds expensive, it often is. Even fairly poor Leos tend to behave as if they have got plenty of money, and those who have don't believe in stinting themselves or others.

Entertaining, Leonine-style

Leo is the sign of fun, pleasure, love and romance. Those born under this sign have a natural *joie de vivre* and know how to enjoy themselves! They enjoy relaxing, going out, visiting the theatre, giving parties and socializing. With their natural ability to enjoy themselves, their warmth, sense of fun, and generosity, they can turn any occasion into a celebration.

Entertaining comes naturally to Leos. They love any chance to dress up and enjoy issuing invitations. Friends who have previously experienced their hospitality are always ready to accept, knowing that they will be looked after in style. Leos are imaginative, and may well have planned an unusual decor or theme for the occasion. One Leo friend of mine hired white doves to decorate his room for a special party; another filled her flat with exotic flowering plants, hired for the event.

Amazing Parties

On a more down-to-earth level, my mother, a typical, warm, imaginative and dramatic Leo, used to give the most amazing parties for my sister and me when we were young. I particularly remember that when we were quite small she made a winding river of shiny green jelly right down the centre of the long table. On top of the river she arranged a flotilla of orange-quarter dinghies with masts made from cocktail sticks and sails of coloured paper. She had – still has – the typical Leonine

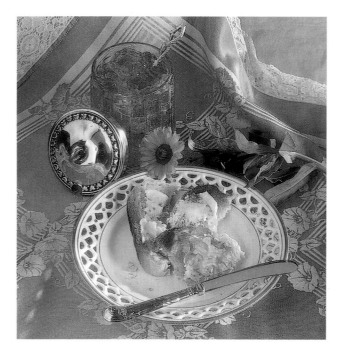

A gift made from a Leonine flower: Marigold Jelly Preserve (page 69)

knack of making an ordinary activity fun. Once, in the days when vegetarianism was still considered peculiar and salads were something you ate occasionally in hot weather, she astounded the occupants of a crowded railway carriage by producing our lunch. This consisted of uncompromisingly wholesome brown sandwiches and huge amounts of salads – Leos always cater generously – including carrot sticks, raw cauliflower and watercress. Eyebrows were raised, heads buried more deeply into newspapers. Completely unabashed, my mother offered the salad around the carriage with a sunny Leonine smile and bright conversation, including the comment: 'We are vegetarian, you know.' She said it, as Leos do, as if it was definitely the right thing to be. Many Leos can involve other people in their schemes simply by their infectious enthusiasm and conviction which breaks down all barriers.

Interesting Ideas

So you may be sure that a Leo's hospitality will be good. There may not always be imported plants or singing birds, but there will be crisp linen, good china, sparkling glass, shining silver, a profusion of fresh flowers and candles and music if appropriate. The food will be good and there will be plenty of it. Leos often cook well and have interesting ideas for flavourings and garnishes but if funds allow, they like to do things in grand style and to hire caterers (the best) or to order gourmet ready-made food from a classy store. They like things to be perfectly presented and they have a gift for delegating jobs – in the most disarming and friendly way – to ensure that everything is just right.

Leos and Health

Leos have a natural vitality and excellent recuperative powers. They do not succumb to long, lingering diseases. If they do become ill, it is usually short and sharp and they burn off infections with a fever. Weak spots are the heart and back, both of which need care. It is vital that Leos watch their diets. They should make sure that apart from the occasional joyful indulgence, they eat plenty of fresh fruit, vegetables and complex carbohydrates such as pasta, bread and rice. They should avoid fats and fatty foods, including – for non-vegetarian Leos – red meat.

Brisk Walks

Some exercise – not necessarily too strenuous – is also good for Leos. Brisk walking is particularly effective and often popular, as is tennis, which is not only physically beneficial but also provides an opportunity for the socializing which Leos love.

A naturally optimistic, hopeful spirit helps any Leo to recover quickly from almost anything. What they cannot take, however, are prolonged periods in dingy, drab surroundings or in an emotionally cold atmosphere where their joyful, loving spirit is not reciprocated and they do not feel appreciated.

Above: Mushrooms in Cream with Saffron Rice; below: Vegetable Lasagne (page 66)

EASY LEMONADE

Quick, easy and refreshing, this is a delicious drink that is particularly pleasant on a hot summer's day – perhaps after tennis, the favourite Leo sport.

Makes 900 ml/1½ pints
1 lemon
25 g/1 oz sugar
6 ice cubes
750 ml/1¼ pints water

Scrub the lemon well under hot water, then cut into rough pieces and place in a blender or food processor. Add the sugar, ice cubes and a little of the measured water. Blend for a few seconds until the lemon is puréed, then strain into a jug and add the remaining water. Serve at once.

MUSHROOMS IN CREAM WITH SAFFRON RICE

Mushrooms are popular with Leos I know. Here they are served as a main course on a base of rice, flavoured with saffron and garnished with bay leaves, herbs of Leo. Culpeper describes saffron as 'an herb of the Sun, and under the Lion, and therefore you need not demand a reason why it strengthens the heart so exceedingly . . . it quicketh the brain . . . it helps consumptions of the lungs and difficulty in breathing'.

Serves 4
750 g/1½ lb button mushrooms
25 g/1 oz butter
2 garlic cloves, crushed
2 tablespoons brandy
1 × 284 ml/10 fl oz carton soured cream
salt and freshly ground black pepper
fresh bay leaves to garnish

For the saffron rice
225 g/8 oz Basmati rice
1½ tablespoons olive oil
1 onion, finely chopped
6 strands of saffron
4 black peppercorns
1 bay leaf
450 ml/¾ pint water
1 teaspoon salt

Start by preparing the saffron rice. Put the Basmati rice into a sieve and wash it under cold water until the water runs completely clear. Shake the sieve thoroughly to get rid of as much water as possible, then leave it on one side to drain.

Heat the olive oil in a medium heavy-bottomed saucepan and add the chopped onion. Cover the saucepan and fry gently for 5 minutes, then add the saffron strands, black peppercorns, bay leaf, reserved rice, measured water and salt. Bring to the boil, then reduce the heat, cover with a tight-fitting lid and leave to cook gently for 20 minutes.

While the rice is cooking, wipe the mushrooms or wash them quickly and dry on absorbent kitchen paper. Cut them into halves or quarters if necessary depending on the size.

Heat the butter without browning in a large saucepan, then add the mushrooms. Cook over high heat for 4 to 5 minutes, stirring often, until tender. Add the crushed garlic cloves and cook for 1 to 2 minutes longer. Add the brandy, then set the brandy alight either with a match or by tipping the pan towards the gas flame. Allow the flames to burn themselves out. Stir in the soured cream and season with salt and freshly ground black pepper. Reheat the mixture gently, but do not allow it to come to the boil.

Arrange the saffron rice around the rim of a large round or oval serving dish and spoon the mushroom and cream mixture into the centre. Serve at once, garnished with fresh bay leaves.

VEGETABLE LASAGNE

The salad burnet snipped all over the top of this adds a refreshing flavour and colour. It is a herb which belongs to Leo, and Culpeper calls it 'a most precious herb – the continual use of it preserves the body in health and the spirit of vigour...' If none is obtainable, chopped fresh parsley or basil make a good substitute.

Serves 4

225-350 g/8-12 oz oven-ready lasagne verde
3-4 tablespoons freshly grated Parmesan cheese
1-2 tablespoons chopped fresh salad burnet (optional),
to garnish
For the vegetable filling
2 tablespoons olive oil
1 large onion, chopped
2 carrots, cut into
5 mm/¼ inch dice
225 g/8 oz courgettes, trimmed and cut into
5 mm/¼ inch dice
1 × 425 g (15 oz) can tomatoes, drained and chopped
100 g/4 oz button mushrooms, wiped and sliced
salt and freshly ground black pepper
For the cream sauce
50 g/2 oz butter
50 g/2 oz plain flour
900 ml/1½ pints milk
1 × 150 ml/5 fl oz carton single cream
freshly grated nutmeg
salt and freshly ground black pepper

Lightly grease a shallow rectangular ovenproof dish and set aside. Make the vegetable filling. Heat the oil in a saucepan, add the onion and carrots, cover the pan and fry for 10 minutes. Add the courgettes, tomatoes and mushrooms, stir well, cover and cook for a further 10 to 15 minutes, or until the vegetables are tender. Season the mixture with salt and pepper.

Meanwhile, make the cream sauce. Melt the butter in a medium saucepan, then add the flour. Stir over the heat for 1 minute, then add a third of the milk. Stir until thick, then stir in another third and stir again. Repeat with the final third, stirring until the sauce is smooth. Leave the sauce to cook over a very gentle heat for 10 minutes, then remove from the heat and stir in the cream, a generous grating of nutmeg and salt and pepper to taste.

Cover the base of the prepared casserole with a thin layer of the cream sauce. Add a layer of lasagne. Spread half the vegetable mixture on top of the lasagne, then add a further layer of cream sauce, using one third of the remaining sauce. Repeat the layers, then finish with a final layer of lasagne followed by the remainder of the cream sauce. Sprinkle with freshly grated Parmesan cheese. Bake the lasagne in a preheated moderate oven, 180°C (350°F), Gas Mark 4 for about 35 minutes. Sprinkle the chopped fresh salad burnet on top, if using, before serving.

RED FRUIT COMPOTE

Although Leos generally prefer dishes made from a single type of fruit or vegetable, this mixture of summer soft fruits is an exception to the rule. All the Leos I know love it.

Serves 4

750 g/1½ lb mixed red fruits (redcurrants,
blackcurrants, raspberries, strawberries)
100 g/4 oz sugar

Remove any stems, then wash the fruit in a sieve. Drain thoroughly and put it into a heavy-bottomed saucepan with the sugar. Cook the fruit over a gentle heat for a few minutes, until the juices run and the sugar has dissolved, stirring often. Remove the pan from the heat and allow to cool. Serve the compote cold, with whipped cream or ice cream and shortbread.

Clockwise from top: Easy Lemonade (page 65); Red Fruit Compote; Lemon Meringue Pie (page 68)

LEMON MERINGUE PIE

The fresh citrus flavours Leos favour make this a pudding they particularly enjoy.

Serves 4-6
wholemeal shortcrust pastry made from 175 g/6 oz flour
(see page 140)
For the filling
4 tablespoons cornflour
300 ml/½ pint water
50 g/2 oz sugar
grated rind and juice of 2 small lemons
25 g/1 oz butter
2 eggs yolks
For the meringue topping
2 egg whites
100 g/4 oz sugar

Roll out the pastry and line a 20 cm/8 in flan dish. Prick the base and bake in a preheated moderately hot oven, 200°C (400°F), Gas Mark 6 for 20 minutes.

Meanwhile make the filling. Put the cornflour into a bowl and blend to a paste with a little of the measured water. Bring the rest of the water to the boil in a saucepan with the sugar. Add to the cornflour paste, stir, then pour it all back into the pan. Add the grated lemon rind and juice and stir over the heat until the mixture has thickened. Remove from the heat and stir in the butter and egg yolks. Pour into the flan case and set aside to cool.

Reduce the oven temperature to moderately hot, 190°C (375°F), Gas Mark 5. Make the meringue topping. In a clean dry bowl, whisk the egg whites until stiff and dry, then whisk in the sugar. Spread the meringue over the top of the lemon mixture, being sure to take it right to the edges (otherwise it goes soggy). Bake in the oven for 35 minutes, until the meringue topping is lightly browned and crisp on the outside. Serve the pie warm or cold.

CHOCOLATE CAKE

I wanted to make a crown-shaped golden marigold cake for Leo, but all the leos I consulted insisted on chocolate cake with fudge icing, so here it is.

Makes one 20 cm/8 inch round cake
200 g/7 oz self-raising 85% wholemeal flour
25 g/1 oz cocoa powder
225 g/8 oz soft butter
225 g/8 oz caster sugar
4 eggs, beaten
For the chocolate fudge filling and topping
75 g/3 oz butter
75 g/3 oz plain chocolate
4 tablespoons milk
225 g/8 oz icing sugar
1 chocolate flake, crumbled

Preheat the oven to moderately hot, 190°C (375°F), Gas Mark 5. Grease two 20 cm/8 inch sandwich tins with butter, then line the base of each with a circle of greased greaseproof paper. Sift the flour and cocoa on to a plate or piece of greaseproof paper. Leave on one side.

Cream the butter and sugar until pale and light. Add the egg 1 teaspoon at a time, beating thoroughly each time to avoid curdling. Then fold in the flour mixture. Spoon the mixture into the tins and level the tops.

Bake, without opening the oven door, for 30 minutes. Test the cake layers by pressing lightly in the centre; the sponge should bounce back. Leave in the tins to cool for 1 minute, then turn out on to a wire rack. Remove the paper, then leave to cool completely.

To make the filling and topping, gently heat the butter, chocolate and milk in a saucepan until melted. Sift in the icing sugar and stir for a móment until well mixed. Cool until beginning to thicken.

Sandwich the cake layers together with half the fudge icing; spread the rest on top. Scatter the pieces of chocolate flake over the top.

GIFTS FOR LEOS

The bright, the dramatic and the luxurious appeal to Leos. They love both quality and quantity and enjoy presents which make them feel pampered. Their colours are gold and the flame colours; also pink; their flowers are sunflowers and marigolds; their gems are diamonds, rubies and cornelians and their metal is gold.

Gold that glisters *Leos love both giving and receiving presents and they are very warm-hearted and generous. They love richly wrapped packages, particularly if they come in shiny gold wrappings (and if the contents are gold, too, for a really special Leo!). They often like pine or lemon-based scents, or exotically warm, spicy ones.*

Cook's choice *For the keen Leo cook, a young bay tree or rosemary shrub in a pot, or some of the Leo flavourings such as saffron, juniper, lovage and burnet. Orange-flower water, walnuts (pickled or fresh), candied orange, lemon or angelica, all of which come under the sign of Leo might also appeal.*

Home-made presents *Leos crave attention and love to feel their family and friends have been thinking of them. Of all the signs, they particularly appreciate something home-made, even if it is quite simple. A jam or preserve, such as the Marigold Jelly Preserve (see below), is perfect. A basket lined with a linen napkin and filled with freshly baked spicy Rock Cakes (see below) would also be ideal.*

MARIGOLD JELLY PRESERVE

Makes about 1 kg/2 lb
1 kg/2 lb cooking apples
750 ml/1¼ pints water
120 ml/4 fl oz lemon juice
4 tablespoons marigold petals
about 750 g/1½ lb sugar
small knob of butter

Wash and quarter the apples. Put them into a large saucepan with 600 ml/1 pint of the measured water and the lemon juice. Cover and cook gently for about 30 minutes. Set a large sieve lined with a piece of muslin or fine cotton over a bowl and pour the apples into the sieve; leave for an hour or so to drip.

Reserve about 1 tablespoon of the marigold petals. Put the rest in a small saucepan with the remaining measured water and simmer gently for 10 minutes, then leave to cool. Strain the marigold water into the apple liquid. Measure all the liquid and pour into a saucepan, adding 350 g/12 oz sugar for every 600 ml/1 pint liquid. Heat over a gentle heat, stirring until the sugar has dissolved, then boil rapidly for about 10 minutes, or until setting point is reached (see page 141). Stir in the butter to disperse the scum, then leave the jelly to stand for 10 to 15 minutes. Pour into hot sterilized jars and cover.

ROCK CAKES

Makes 24
225 g/8 oz self-raising wholemeal flour
½ teaspoon cinnamon
½ teaspoon mixed spice
75 g/3 oz butter
100 g/4 oz sugar
25 g/1 oz currants
25 g/1 oz sultanas
25 g/1 oz chopped mixed peel
1 egg
4-5 tablespoons milk
a little demerara sugar for topping

Preheat the oven to moderately hot, 200°C (400°F), Gas Mark 6. Lightly grease a large baking sheet. Sift the flour and spice into a mixing bowl, tipping in any bran left in the sieve. Rub in the butter until the mixture resembles fine breadcrumbs. Add the sugar and dried fruits and mix in well. In a second bowl, beat the egg and add the milk, then pour these on to the dry ingredients and mix to a stiff dough. Place heaped tablespoons of the mixture on the baking sheet and sprinkle with demerara sugar. Bake for 10 to 15 minutes or until golden brown. Cool on a wire rack.

VIRGO

Virgo – the 'discriminating eater' – belongs to the Earth element like Taurus and Capricorn, and people born under this sign are realistic, reliable and down-to-earth. They are excellent planners, well prepared for emergencies, calm and collected at times of crisis. They enjoy practical activities, crafts and making things with their hands, particularly if these pastimes call for ingenuity and thrift. Virgoans are also naturally good at caring for others because they are kind yet firm, practical and unemotional. They are interested in health, hygiene, nutrition and healing, and often know a great deal about vitamins and remedies.

The sign of Virgo is not, however, as straightforward as you might imagine. This is because it belongs to the Mutable group of signs, along with Gemini, Sagittarius and Pisces, and this makes Virgoans much more changeable, versatile and intellectual than their element, Earth, would otherwise suggest. In addition, their ruling planet is Mercury, planet of the mind, intelligence and communication.

Natural Students

This combination means that Virgoans can use their minds in practical ways. They have a naturally scientific bent, excellent powers of criticism and discrimination. Virgoans are ingenious, inventive and curious. They are natural students and researchers and enjoy collecting and organizing information.

Most Virgoans are well-read, love books and have a well-stocked library. They particularly like reference books and encyclopaedias. They are often drawn to clerical and secretarial work and have natural gifts in

this direction. They have an excellent business sense, generally erring on the side of caution.

Virgo is the sign of the perfectionist, and people born under this sign have high standards both for themselves and for others. They are hardworking and conscientious and sometimes it seems as if they are constantly striving towards an impossible goal. Because they are so aware of their own shortcomings, Virgoans are modest, even casual and dismissive, about their achievements.

I have certainly found this with my Virgoan daughter. She is very clever, but when she has been successful, she never comes bursting into the house, full of triumph, but tells me quietly, after a while, in an almost matter-of-fact way, pleased yet totally unassuming.

Missed Opportunities

Realistic both about their own abilities and of the demands of the tasks ahead of them, Virgoans do not push themselves forward and as a result may miss opportunities seized by those born under the more enthusiastic yet less able signs. Positive thought, creative visualization and affirmations can help Virgoans.

The warmth and support of friends also mean a great deal, yet Virgoans often feel that others are critical of them. When this happens, it is usually a case of like begets like. If a Virgoan can curb a sharp tongue, look for the positive and be warm and generous in praise, the situation will improve.

High Standards

In relationships, Virgoans may appear reserved and find it difficult to make the first move. Their tendency to be critical, coupled with their high standards, can also make them seem much more cool and aloof than they really are. In fact, Virgoans are warm-hearted and kind and will respond with touching enthusiasm if you reach out to them. I have found that Virgoans long for affection but find it extremely difficult to be demonstrative, so other signs need to make the first move and give a Virgoan a hug!

The symbol of Virgo is the virgin, which expresses the feeling which Virgoans have for wholeness and purity in their lives. They care about naturalness, health, cleanliness and the environment. They are usually fussy about the kind of clothes they wear (many will choose only natural fibres), the foods they eat (natural again) and the places at which they shop.

Successful

The Virgoan combination of intelligence, adaptability and practicality, together with reliability, means that they succeed in many jobs. If they can also cultivate warmth, confidence and the ability to take risks, the sky's the limit! They are especially drawn to work which makes use of their skill in dealing with details: bookkeeping, accountancy, work with statistics and analysis, secretarial, editorial or clerical work or literary criticism. They also make good teachers, lecturers and broadcasters once they have overcome their natural shyness.

A career in the area of health and diet often interests a Virgoan, and many excellent nurses, doctors and healers are born under this sign.

Foods for Virgoans

Virgoans are as discriminating about the foods they buy and eat as about every other aspect of their lives. They seek purity and naturalness, will put cleanliness and efficiency high on the list when choosing a food shop and will read labels carefully.

Because of their interest in health, and their high standards, Virgoans may sometimes be picky eaters. Yet they enjoy good, natural food, simply prepared and honestly presented, without fussy, over-rich sauces – one accompaniment they do enjoy, though, are pickled onions. Their choice of fresh produce (which they will always buy in preference to frozen or canned) and for top-quality ingredients such as the very best butter, top quality wine vinegar and cold-pressed virgin olive oil, means that their food always tastes good.

Methodical and Meticulous

Virgoans shop, as they cook, methodically, using a list meticulously. In the supermarket, my Virgoan daughter put me right on my easy-going ways: ingredients for the refrigerator had to be put into one carrier bag, cans in another, dried goods in a third – my shopping has never been the same since!

In the kitchen, a Virgoan usually works cleanly and methodically and will follow a recipe accurately. They like to collect the best equipment, and here again their preference for natural materials is evident in the choice of wood, pottery and earthenware bowls and casseroles, usually in soft, understated colours.

Salad Lovers

Virgoans like food simply cooked, prepared in healthy ways. They grill, bake or stir-fry rather than fry, lightly steam rather than boil their vegetables and make dressings and toppings from low-fat yogurt rather than cream. They prefer luscious fresh fruit desserts to sweet, rich puddings. Many Virgoans love crisp, crunchy salads, perhaps flavoured with the herbs of their sign, dill, savory, fresh marjoram or parsley.

Foods which come under Virgo are all those which belong to Mercury and include carrots, celery, fennel and mulberries, with parsley, caraway, fennel, dill, marjoram, oregano and lavender for flavouring. Culpeper would recommend that Virgoans of a highly strung nature should take also the soothing foods of the Moon and Venus, and, to build up their courage, the invigorating foods of Mars such as onions and warming spices. Foods rich in B vitamins are particularly good for

A dainty gift for the tidy Virgoan: Cookie Jar (page 79)

Virgoans. Wholewheat bread and whole grains, wheatgerm and pulses (which are all astrologically attributed to Venus) and yeast and yogurt (which come under the Moon) are beneficial to the nervous system and should be supplemented with plenty of fresh fruit and vegetables.

Entertaining, Virgoan-style

Virgoans entertain meticulously. They will issue precise invitations and hate it if guests are late. The house will be clean and shining and fragrant with fresh flowers, perhaps lavender, lilies of the valley or delicate ferns, which all belong to Virgo.

Because of their high standards, Virgoans find entertaining something of a strain. They need to get everything ready in advance. Only then will they relax and enjoy the party, trusting to the spirit of the occasion to ensure that everything turns out successfully.

Eating Out

Virgoans enjoy eating out, though they often suspect that their own cooking is better than the chef's, and may feel slightly uncomfortable not knowing exactly what is in the dishes, how fresh the ingredients were, and whether the kitchen was Virgo-clean. Virgoans have been known to take to restaurants little bottles containing salt-free, additive-free salad dressing or dairy-free milk substitute, but I think this is going too far!

Virgoans and Health

Virgo is the most health-conscious sign of the Zodiac. The Virgo house in the horoscope is the one which shows health, which is why people born under this sign are usually interested in fitness, health, diet, healing and hygiene. As a result, they usually take good care of themselves and their families.

This interest, plus their natural tendency to anxiety and caution, may lead to excessive concern about health matters. Virgoans are highly strung, owing to the Mutability of the sign and the influence of Mercury, though they might deny this. The stresses and strains of their life, plus their natural tendency to worry, can affect their health.

Letting Go

Virgoans can help themselves greatly by relaxing, just letting go of worries, trusting that all will be well and gently becoming more positive in outlook. Meditation can be very helpful to Virgoans.

The parts of the body ruled by Virgo are the intestines, abdomen and hands (which are also ruled by Gemini, the other sign with Mercury as its ruling planet). Many Virgoans find that their nerves go straight to their stomach, and they suffer from various forms of indigestion. Relaxation, a calm mental attitude, and eating light, healthy foods, will all help. A diet rich in natural fibre is particularly important for Virgoans.

Clockwise from top: Celery, Orange and Watercress Salad; Tiger's Milk (page 78); Wholewheat Vegetable Tartlets

SORREL SOUP

According to Culpeper, sorrel soup brings the soothing qualities of Venus and will 'refresh the overspent spirits . . . quench thirst, and procure an appetite'.

Serves 4
40 g/1½ oz butter
1 onion, chopped
2 potatoes, diced
1 litre/1¾ pints water
75 g/3 oz sorrel leaves, washed
3-4 tablespoons single cream
salt and freshly ground black pepper
freshly grated nutmeg
pinch of sugar

Melt the butter in a large saucepan and fry the onion gently for 5 minutes. Add the potato, cover the pan and cook for a further 5 to 10 minutes, without browning.

Stir in the water, bring to the boil, then simmer for about 15 minutes until the potato is tender. Purée in a blender or food processor with the sorrel and cream. Reheat gently, but do not boil. Season to taste with salt, pepper, nutmeg and sugar. Serve hot or chilled.

CELERY, ORANGE AND WATERCRESS SALAD

Here a Virgoan ingredient, celery, combines with glowing oranges from the Sun and watercress from fiery Mars to make a salad which is popular with one of my favourite Virgoans. The salad makes a health-giving light lunch or a refreshing first course.

Serves 2
1 celery heart, chopped
2 small oranges, peeled and sliced into rounds
½ bunch watercress

For the dressing
50 g/2 oz Danish blue or Roquefort cheese, crumbled
4 tablespoons soured cream or plain yogurt

Arrange the celery, orange slices and watercress attractively on 2 plates. Mix together the cheese and soured cream. Pour the dressing over the top of the salad, but do not mask it completely. Serve at once.

WHOLEWHEAT VEGETABLE TARTLETS

Serves 4
175 g/6 oz plain wholemeal flour
75 g/3 oz butter
1-2 tablespoons cold water
For the filling
2 eggs, beaten
175 g/6 oz frozen mixed vegetables
1 × 150 ml/5 fl oz carton single cream
salt and freshly ground black pepper
40-50 g/1½-2 oz grated Cheddar cheese

Preheat the oven to moderate, 180°C (350°F), Gas Mark 4. Sift the flour into a bowl, also adding the bran from the sieve. Rub in the butter until the mixture resembles fine breadcrumbs and add enough water to make a dough. Divide into four equal pieces and roll each out to fit a 10 cm/4 inch flan tin; trim the edges, prick the bases, then bake for about 15 minutes, until set.

Remove the tartlets from the oven, then brush the bases generously with beaten egg, making sure all the fork holes are sealed. Return the tartlets to the oven and bake for about 5 minutes, until the egg is set. Remove from the oven. Spoon some of the raw vegetables into each flan. Add the cream to the remaining egg in a bowl, season, then pour over the vegetables and sprinkle with cheese. Bake for 15 minutes, or until the flans are set and golden brown. Serve hot or warm.

LENTIL ROAST

This is one of the simplest lentil recipes I know. I serve it with crisp roast potatoes, fresh vegetables in season, such as carrots and broccoli, a vegetarian gravy (see page 105) and redcurrant or mulberry jelly.

Serves 6
500 g/1 lb split red lentils
450 ml/15 fl oz water
25 g/1 oz butter or 2 tablespoons sunflower oil
2 large onions, chopped
1 teaspoon dried thyme or mixed herbs
4 tablespoons lemon juice
salt and freshly ground black pepper
a little wholemeal flour for coating
a little oil for roasting
sprigs of parsley and lemon slices to garnish

Put the lentils into a heavy-bottomed saucepan with the measured water; bring to the boil, then turn the heat down as low as possible and cover the pan. Cook for 20 to 30 minutes, stirring occasionally, until all the lentils are soft and sand-coloured. They should be very dry. Set aside. Heat the butter in a saucepan, add the onions. Cover and fry for 10 minutes, until soft but not browned. Tip the onion into a bowl and add the lentils, herbs, lemon juice and seasoning. Press the mixture together, then turn out on to a floured board and shape into a roll. Coat lightly in wholemeal flour.

Pour a little oil – to a depth of about 3 mm/⅛ inch – into a Swiss roll tin or roasting tin big enough to hold the roast. Put the tin into the oven to heat up. When the oil is smoking hot, carefully add the roll to it. Turn it gently, to coat both sides with oil. Bake near the top of the oven for 45 minutes, until golden and crisp, spooning a little oil over the roast from time to time. Drain the cooked roll, transfer to a large warm serving dish, garnish with parsley and lemon slices and serve as suggested above.

LAVENDER CAKE

Makes one 20 cm/8 inch round cake
4 eggs
100 g/4 oz lavender sugar or caster sugar and a few drops of oil of lavender
100 g/4 oz plain flour
pinch of salt
For the filling and icing
50 g/2 oz unsalted butter
225 g/8 oz lavender icing sugar, or icing sugar and a few drops of oil of lavender
a few drops of red and blue food colouring
crystallized lavender flowers (see page 141) to decorate

Line the base of two 20 cm/8 inch sandwich tins with greased greaseproof paper. Beat the eggs and sugar with an electric beater for about 5 minutes until very pale and doubled in bulk. A little of the mixture, flicked on top of the rest, should leave a trail. Alternatively, combine in a heatproof bowl set over a saucepan of gently simmering water (the bowl should not touch the water) and whisk. Cool, whisking occasionally.

Preheat the oven to moderate, 180°C (350°F), Gas Mark 4. Sift the flour and salt on to the egg mixture. Using a metal spoon, fold in gently but thoroughly. Pour the mixture into the tins. Bake for 30 to 35 minutes, or until the cakes have shrunk from the sides of the tins and spring back when touched in the centre. Cool in the tins for 2 to 3 minutes, turn out on to a wire rack, remove the paper and leave to cool completely.

Cream the butter with half the icing sugar, adding a few drops of hot water, if necessary, for a spreading consistency. Use to sandwich the layers together.

To make the icing, put the rest of the icing sugar into a bowl and stir in 1 to 2 tablespoons of water, to make a pouring consistency. Tint pale mauve with a few drops of red and blue food colouring. Pour the icing over the top of the cake so that it just flows to the edges. Decorate with crystallized lavender flowers.

Clockwise from top: Lavender Cake; Wholemeal Caraway Plait (page 78); Mulberry Jam (page 79)

WHOLEMEAL CARAWAY PLAIT

Caraway is one of Virgo's plants, being traditionally attributed to its ruling planet, Mercury. Culpeper considers caraway to be 'conducing to all cold griefs of the head and stomach, bowels... as also the wind in them, and helpeth to sharpen the eyesight...' Caraway has a pleasing flavour, reminiscent of aniseed, but other seeds such as sesame or poppy may be substituted if preferred.

Makes 2 plaits
15 g/½ oz dried yeast
1 tablespoon brown sugar
450 ml/¾ pint tepid water
750 g/1½ lb wholemeal flour
15 g/½ oz butter or margarine
1½ teaspoons salt
For the glaze and topping
1 small egg beaten with ¼ teaspoon salt
2 teaspoons caraway seeds

Put the dried yeast into a jug with ½ teaspoon of the brown sugar. Add two thirds of the measured water and mix in well with a fork. Set aside in a warm place for about 10 to 15 minutes, until the mixture has become very frothy.

Meanwhile put the wholemeal flour into a large bowl and rub in the butter or margarine. Stir the remaining sugar, with the salt, into the remaining water. Add to the flour, together with the frothy yeast mixture. Mix, adding a little more warm water if necessary, until a pliable dough is formed. Then turn the dough out on a clean work surface and knead the dough for about 5 minutes, until it is smooth. Transfer the dough to a large, oiled bowl, cover with oiled polythene, and set aside in a warm place to prove for about 45 minutes, or until the dough has doubled in bulk. Preheat the oven to hot, 230°C (450°F), Gas Mark 8.

Turn the risen dough out on to a clean work surface and knead briefly, then divide it in half. Divide one of the halves further into three equal pieces, then roll each to a 36 cm/14 inch sausage with a bulge in the middle. Join the three pieces together at one end, then plait them, joining them at the other end. Tuck under the ends, then make another plait with the remaining dough in exactly the same way.

Brush the plaits with the beaten egg glaze and sprinkle with caraway seeds. Place them well apart on a greased baking sheet and set aside in a warm place for about 20 minutes until they are well risen. Bake in the oven for 20 minutes, then reduce the oven temperature to moderately hot, 200°C (400°F), Gas Mark 6 and bake for a further 15 minutes. The bases of the loaves should sound hollow when tapped. Transfer the loaves to a wire rack and leave to cool.

TIGER'S MILK

Culpeper didn't assign chufa or tiger nuts to any planet, but I think he would have given them to Venus, along with groundnuts. They have the soothing qualities of that planet, and may be made into a nourishing and sustaining drink which appeals to Virgoans when they do not feel like eating. You can buy tiger nuts or chufa nuts, which are small rhizomes, at health shops and in some supermarkets.

Makes about 700 ml/1¼ pints
225 g/8 oz chufa or tiger nuts
1 litre/1¾ pints water
lemon zest, cinnamon, sugar or honey (optional)

Wash the chufa or tiger nuts thoroughly, then purée them in a blender or food processor with the measured water. Pour the mixture into a jug and leave to stand for 3 to 4 hours, liquidize again, then strain and chill. The milk may be flavoured with lemon zest or with a little cinnamon and a dash of sugar or honey.

GIFTS FOR VIRGOANS

The neat, the clean, and the clever appeal to Virgoans; they often like miniature items provided they are well-made and of the best quality. Their colours are white, blue and grey; their flowers are ferns, lilies of the valley, honeysuckle and lavender; their gems are topaz, hyacinth, pink jasper, peridot and sardonyx and their metal is mercury.

Files and facts *Any stationery appeals to a Virgoan, especially things like files with alphabetical dividers or photograph albums. They also enjoy books of information such as encyclopaedias, and gifts which help them to be clean and organized, like a stand and cover for a recipe book.*

Honey and home-made jam *Food-wise, some Virgoans would love to be spoiled with exclusive chocolates and fine wines, but unless you know them well, you're safer with real comb honey or home-made pickled onions or preserves, such as the mulberry jam below.*

Fragrance and flowers *It is dodgy giving Virgoans scented gifts, even soap, since they may well prefer unperfumed varieties. Those who like perfume are usually drawn to lavender and lily of the valley. They would probably enjoy a pot plant or dried flowers, a little bonsai tree, a miniature orange plant or a book about growing plants from seed.*

MULBERRY JAM

'Mercury rules the tree, therefore its effects are as variable as his are... The juice or the syrup made of the juice of the berries, helpeth all inflammations or sores in the mouth or throat...' That was Culpeper's pronouncement on mulberries. If you cannot get mulberries, use loganberries, raspberries or tayberries.

Makes about 2.3 kg/5 lb
1.5 kg/3 lb mulberries
600 ml/1 pint water
500 g/1 lb peeled, cored and sliced cooking apples
1.6 kg/3½ lb sugar
knob of butter

Place the mulberries in a preserving pan with half the measured water and simmer gently for about 20 minutes until soft and pulpy. Meanwhile place the apples in a saucepan with the remaining water and simmer gently for about 20 minutes. Add the apples to the mulberries and stir in the sugar. Continue stirring until the sugar has dissolved, then add the knob of butter.

Bring to the boil and boil rapidly for about 10 minutes, stirring frequently. When setting point is reached (see page 141), remove the pan from the heat and skim off any scum. Spoon into clean, warm sterilized jars and cover.

COOKIE JAR

A jar of these dainty cookies would appeal to the fastidious Virgoan, and make an ideal gift.

Makes 40-50 cookies
100 g/4 oz butter
25 g/1 oz icing sugar
100 g/4 oz plain flour
pinch of baking powder
vanilla essence
icing sugar, glacé cherries, walnut pieces,
melted chocolate, to decorate

Preheat the oven to moderately hot, 190°C (375°F), Gas Mark 5. Place the butter in a mixing bowl and cream until soft and light, then add the icing sugar and beat until fluffy. Sift the flour and baking powder on top, then mix in thoroughly, adding a few drops of vanilla essence.

Put the mixture into a piping bag fitted with a medium shell nozzle. Pipe circles and fingers on to greased baking sheets, allowing room for spreading. Placed halved glacé cherries on some and pieces of walnut on others, leaving some plain.

Bake for 15 to 20 minutes, until set and golden brown. Cool on a wire rack. Dip some of the biscuits in melted chocolate and sift icing sugar over others. When the chocolate has firmed, put the cookies into a clean, dry airtight jar.

LIBRA

Charmer of the zodiac, peacemaker and devil's advocate, Libra – the 'sociable eater' – belongs to the Air group of signs and is of Cardinal quality. It is symbolized by a pair of scales and ruled by the planet of love, beauty and harmony, Venus.

All these factors are reflected in the Libran personality. Like all air signs, Librans are light, amusing and cultured, with bright, clever and enquiring minds. They love good conversation, books and music, and are likely to be found in bookshops, art galleries, theatres or at concerts. The Air element emphasizes the mind and intellect, and the other Air signs, Gemini and Aquarius, tend to be so caught up with ideas and activities that they are not particularly interested in eating (unless their Moon or rising sign favours food). In the case of Libra, however, while the Air brings intelligence, detachment and refinement, the influence of Venus gives a very definite love of food, not to mention beauty, pleasure and luxury.

Librans – like people born under the other sign ruled by Venus, Taurus – have a real appreciation of anything to do with the senses and they really know how to enjoy themselves. They are often found in jobs connected with the Arts, or with music, publishing or the beauty business; or in work in which their attractive appearance and manner is an asset.

Balanced View

Libra's symbol, the scales, gives further clues to the Libran personality. Balance is essential to people born under this sign. They like to feel that they are taking a just and balanced view of any situation; they consider themselves fair. Hence they are often slow to make up their minds, weighing up each side in trying to reach the perfect answer. Once they have come to a decision, however, they can be determined, courageous and strong-minded.

If you want to get the best out of a Libran, give him time, never rush him. Librans, incidentally, will seldom appear to be hurried; even when they are working extremely hard, they have an air of calm and poise which may well be the reason for their 'lazy Libra' nickname. This is (mostly) unjustified; Librans will work as hard as any of the signs, harder and with more determination than some. It is just that they also know, better than almost any other signs except perhaps Leo and Taurus, how to enjoy themselves...

Diplomatic Touch

Librans have the reputation for being the peacemakers of the zodiac and they can certainly bring their pleasant manner and air of detachment to ease an awkward situation. Their ability to see both sides, their fairness and their diplomacy make Librans natural peacemakers. That is not to say they don't enjoy an argument, and if things become too static, they will certainly throw out a well-timed verbal firework to liven things up. If they feel that a discussion is too heavily biased, they will have no hesitation in putting the opposite point of view, even if this causes sparks to fly.

Foods for Librans

Librans love food. The influence of their ruling planet, sensual, pleasure-loving Venus, means that most foods appeal, and selecting the recipes for this sign was difficult. Foods which have a particular appeal are those which are light, creamy, and delicately seasoned.

They also like dishes which incorporate plenty of their element, air. Soufflés, meringues, ice creams, syllabubs, and light, whisked sponge cakes are all Libran favourites. They find sweets difficult to resist, particularly the pretty coloured ones like sugared almonds.

Librans feast with their eyes as well as with their palates, and they like foods to look attractive and to be presented properly. All the Librans I know love Oriental food – especially Japanese – with its emphasis on colour and presentation. Nouvelle cuisine often appeals to Librans for the same reason; they enjoy several small, perfectly presented courses, and miniature dishes such as tiny flans, cocktail canapés or little cakes iced in toning pastel colours.

Demi-vegetarians

Librans are not generally big meat-eaters, and some are vegetarian for aesthetic reasons, though they are more likely to be 'demi-vegetarians', following their instinct for balance and their tendency to be easy-going.

Food shopping is a task Librans enjoy, seeking out the best quality, comparing prices, weighing up the pros and cons of each purchase. They particularly like visiting the delicatessen, with its colourful array, and they will often buy ready-made gourmet dishes. Librans always choose the best; they will not tolerate artificial flavours or colours, and will go out of their way to buy their bread from the best baker in town. Freshly roasted coffee beans are a priority as are the finest tea and the best first-pressing olive oil. If this sounds expensive, it is! Librans do not penny-pinch and can be quite extravagant, though their natural sense of balance means that a particularly excessive spending-spree is usually followed by a period of thrift. But this is not easy for them!

Fresh Fruit

Since Venus rules Libra, all the Venusian ingredients belong to this sign, giving a wide range to choose from. Fruits such as peaches, apricots, pears, apples, plums, cherries, blackberries, grapes, gooseberries, strawberries and raspberries; vegetables including all types of bean, peas, tomatoes, potatoes, parsnips, endive, avocado pears; wheat and all products made from this grain. For flavouring, select the classic Venusian herbs of mint, thyme, sorrel, and lovage. Another herb which comes under Venus and which could be particularly useful for Librans is feverfew, which has been found, in some cases, to help the migraines which may beset Librans from time to time. Burdock, another herb traditionally under this sign, is a herbal remedy for kidney problems, to which, again, Librans may be susceptible.

Other foods which, according to Culpeper, are good for Librans, because they supply the toning and bracing Martian quality, which complements the gentle Venus, are onions, garlic, leeks, shallots, mustard, horseradish and hot vegetables such as watercress and rocket. Nettles, which also come under Mars, are a well-known herbal remedy for kidney problems.

Entertaining, Libran-style

Sociable, tasteful and generous, Librans love to entertain and do so with great flair, whether it is a drinks party with champagne and canapés, an elegant dinner with soft music and witty conversation or an intimate, romantic supper for two.

For an informal but delectable meal a Libran might serve as a starter a selection of Italian antipasti with juicy olives, or steamed fresh asparagus with butter, or perfect avocados with an excellent home-made vinaigrette. To follow, perhaps pasta con pesto with a tomato salad (or one made with a selection of lettuce leaves of different colours) and a perfect vinaigrette. Then a carefully chosen cheese board, possibly featuring an interesting new cheese, with a velvet-smooth sorbet or ice cream, or perhaps a light-as-air gateau, to round off the meal. Naturally the wines would complement the

For the luxury-loving Libran: hand-made Chocoloate Truffles (page 89)

food, the scene would be set by soft music, a pastel cloth, crisply laundered linen napkins and toning flowers.

Librans and Health

The key to good health for Librans lies in balance, and the fact that their symbol is the scales does not mean that they find this easy to achieve. They are constantly striving for poise and perfection, both in their everyday life and where their health is concerned. In the process, their moods fluctuate and this influences their flow of vitality.

Libra is one of the most companionable and sociable of signs, and although Librans may appear detached and independent, few Librans are truly happy without a mate. This is part of their search for balance: they need someone to complement them.

Sense of Balance

Librans tend to fluctuate in weight at the best of times – that balancing act again – but a natural sense of moderation prevents most Librans from going too far in either direction. A spell of overindulgence will be almost automatically followed by a period of austerity, just as exertion and late nights will lead to extra rest. This natural process of correction helps most Librans to keep in good health.

Beauty and harmony are extremely important to Librans and they cannot be happy or healthy for long in a coarse, ugly or harsh environment. Attractive surroundings with harmonizing colours, pleasant music, and comfortable furniture help a Libran to feel tranquil, healthy and happy. The opposite situation can have an adverse effect and bring on illnesses such as headaches, back pains, eczema and other skin problems.

Vulnerable Spots

The parts of the body traditionally ruled by Libra are the kidneys and the renal system, and the lower back or lumbar region. These may be vulnerable areas, and Librans would be well-advised to watch their intake of alcohol because of its effect on the kidneys. It is preferable to drink plenty of clear pure water. Librans must also be careful when it comes to their craving for sweet foods – they certainly don't need any extra encouragement here!

The Libran love of sugar can make those born under the sign particularly susceptible to excess weight. A good diet can make a great deal of difference. When slimming, Librans are probably most likely to succeed with a classic, calorie-controlled diet because it enables them to pick and choose what they eat, and to include some sweet treats. A day or two on just one type of fruit, particularly apples, grapes or strawberries, can be very helpful to cleanse the system, enable the Libran to shed a few pounds quickly and break bad eating habits at the beginning of the diet, or re-establish routine after a spell of overindulgence.

Above: Roasted Cashew Nut Roulade with Asparagus Filling (page 86); below: Libran Canapés

LIBRAN CANAPÉS

Librans enjoy dainty morsels, prettily decorated, and love to offer friends and guests a colourful selection of tasty canapés. Arrange all or a selection of the following attractively on a tray or large platter, perhaps lined with fresh mint leaves and decorated with spring onion curls and radish roses.

Fruit and cheese kebabs For these you will need 250 g/9 oz cheese (75 g/3 oz of each of 3 different types, such as white cheese with walnuts, Cheddar cheese with red wine, sage Derby or Cotswold) cut into about 72 cubes, and assorted fruits, as interesting as possible, such as whole seedless grapes, pieces of ripe apricot, mango, pawpaw, lychee, apple or kiwi fruit, to make about 350 g/12 oz of bite-sized pieces, and 24 cocktail sticks. Thread the cheese and fruit alternately on to the cocktail sticks, using 3 types of cheese for each cocktail stick, and 3 pieces of fruit.

Stuffed cherry tomatoes Cut the tops off the tomatoes and level the bases too, if necessary, to enable the tomatoes to stand upright. Carefully scoop out the seeds with a small teaspoon, then spoon or pipe curd cheese into the tomato cavities. You will need 175 g/6 oz curd cheese for 24 tomatoes.

Stuffed dates with cream cheese and mint Remove the stones from fresh dates, and fill each with a little cream cheese and 1 fresh mint leaf. For 24 fresh dates you will need the same number of fresh mint leaves and 175 g/ 6 oz cream cheese.

Cream cheese balls Form curd cheese into even-sized balls about the size of large marbles. Roll ⅓ of the curd cheese balls in crushed roasted peanuts, another ⅓ in chopped chives and the rest in very finely chopped red pepper. For 32 balls you will need about 450 g/1 lb curd cheese.

Miniature quiches Cut circles of shortcrust pastry to fit a miniature tartlet tin, prick lightly and bake in a preheated moderately hot oven, 200°C (400°F), Gas Mark 6 for about 10 minutes until set. Remove from the oven, and brush each with beaten egg. Return the quiches to the oven for 5 minutes, until lightly browned, then cool. For 30 miniature quiches you will need about 12 oz shortcrust pastry and 1 egg, lightly beaten.

Fill with pretty, tasty mixtures such as mayonnaise and a tiny asparagus tip; potato salad, coloured palest pink with beetroot juice and decorated with a slice of radish and a sprig of dill; avocado dip and a slice of stuffed olive; curd cheese and a halved grape; hummus, a sprinkling of paprika and a piece of black olive.

CHINESE VEGETABLE STIR-FRY

The Librans I know love Oriental food. A stir-fry like this is not only beautiful to look at and delicious to eat, but it is also extremely quick and easy to make, which suits a Libran admirably!

Serves 4
2 tablespoons vegetable oil
1 onion, sliced
1 garlic clove, crushed
1 bunch of spring onions, trimmed
225 g/8 oz baby sweetcorn, trimmed
225 g/8 oz mangetout
350 g/12 oz beansprouts
225 g/8 oz button mushrooms or 1 × 425 g/15 oz jar of
Chinese straw mushrooms
2 tablespoons soy sauce
boiled rice to serve

Prepare all the vegetables. Just before serving, heat the oil in a large saucepan or wok and fry the onion for 4 to 5 minutes. Then add the garlic, spring onions, sweetcorn, mangetout, beansprouts and mushrooms. Stir-fry over a high heat for 3 to 4 minutes, until all the vegetables are heated through, then stir in the soy sauce and serve at once.

ROASTED CASHEW NUT ROULADE WITH ASPARAGUS FILLING

Serves 6
4 large eggs
salt and freshly ground black pepper
175 g/6 oz roasted cashew nuts, crushed
For the filling
350 g/12 oz fresh asparagus, trimmed
1 × 284 ml/10 fl oz carton soured cream
salt and freshly ground black pepper

Preheat the oven to moderately hot, 200°C (400°F), Gas Mark 6. Line a 33 × 23 cm/13 × 9 inch Swiss roll tin with buttered greaseproof paper, letting it extend 5 cm/2 inches above the edge of the tin and snipping it diagonally into the corners.

Cook the asparagus, either by placing the spears in a steamer, or by boiling them in water to cover, for 6 to 8 minutes. Remove from the steamer or water as soon as they are done. Cut the tips from the stems and set aside; chop the stems and reserve separately.

Make the roulade. In a large bowl, whisk the eggs with the salt and pepper until thick. Fold in half the cashew nuts and pour into the tin, spreading evenly into the corners. Bake near the top of the oven for 6 to 8 minutes, until firm in the centre. Soak a clean tea towel in cold water, wring it thoroughly, then place on a flat surface. Cover with a piece of greaseproof paper spread with the remaining cashew nuts. Invert the roulade on to the nuts and remove the base paper.

Place the soured cream in a bowl and mix with the chopped asparagus. Season and spread over the roulade. Distribute all but six of the asparagus tips on top. Roll up the roulade by folding one long side into the centre and the other on top. Place a large oiled piece of foil on top and turn the roulade upside down. Slide a baking sheet under and remove the paper and cloth. Bring up the sides of the foil to enclose the roulade.

Reheat immediately or when required (still wrapped in foil) in a preheated moderately hot oven, 190°C (375°F), Gas Mark 5, for 15 to 20 minutes. Remove the foil and transfer the roulade to an oval plate. Arrange the asparagus tips on top and serve at once.

JEWEL CAKES

Makes about 36
butter for greasing
2 eggs
50 g/2 oz caster sugar
50 g/2 oz unbleached white flour
a pinch of salt
For the icing and decorations
apricot jam
50 g/2 oz almond paste
225 g/8 oz icing sugar
cake colourings in assorted colours
chocolate flake, mimosa balls, glacé cherries, angelica,
nuts and crystallized flowers to decorate

Grease and base-line a 20 cm/7 inch square tin. Preheat the oven to moderate, 180°C (350°F), Gas Mark 4. Using the eggs, sugar, flour and salt, make a sponge cake mixture, following the method for Airy Violet Cake (see page 88). Pour into the tin. Bake for 15 to 20 minutes, or until the mixture has shrunk from the sides and springs back when touched lightly in the centre. Cool for 2 to 3 minutes in the tin, then turn on to a wire rack and peel off the lining paper. Set aside until cold.

Cut into small shapes about 4 cm/1½ inches in size. Heat the jam and brush over the shapes. Roll small pieces of almond paste into a ball and place on top.

Mix the icing sugar with a little water, then divide into five portions. Colour four in pastel shades. Spoon the icing over the cakes, covering completely.

Pipe lines, dots, curls and flowers in contrasting colours on top of the cakes if you wish and decorate with chocolate flake, mimosa balls etc as desired.

Above: Airy Violet Cake (page 88); Jewel Cakes

AIRY VIOLET CAKE

The violet, Culpeper's 'fine pleasing flower of Venus' is said to soothe many ills. It 'easeth pains in the head caused through want of sleep'. Here it is used both for flavouring and decorating a cake which is as light and lovely as the Libran temperament.

Makes one 20 cm/8 inch round cake
butter for greasing
4 eggs
100 g/4 oz caster sugar
100 g/4 oz plain unbleached white flour
a pinch of salt
For the filling and topping
1 × 150 ml/5 fl oz carton double cream
a few drops of violet essence
1-2 tablespoons caster sugar
1-2 tablespoons water
175 g/6 oz icing sugar
crystallized violets to decorate (see page 141)

Grease and base-line two 20 cm/8 inch sandwich tins. Combine the eggs and sugar in a bowl and whisk together until the mixture is very pale, has doubled in bulk and leaves a trail on the surface when the whisk is lifted. This will take about 5 minutes with an electric whisk. By hand, whisking will take about 15 minutes, and the bowl should be placed over a saucepan of simmering water (avoid letting the bowl touch the water). Allow the mixture to cool, whisking from time to time.

Preheat the oven to moderate, 180°C (350°F), Gas Mark 4. Sift the flour and salt on top of the egg mixture, then gently fold in using a metal spoon. Pour into the tins. Bake for 30 to 35 minutes, or until the cakes have shrunk from the sides and spring back when touched in the centre. Cool for 2 to 3 minutes in the tins, then turn on to a wire rack and peel off the lining paper.

Allow the cakes to get completely cold, then decorate.

Whip the cream until stiff, adding violet essence and caster sugar. Sandwich the cakes with this cream.

Add a little violet essence and enough water to the icing sugar to make a soft icing. Spread over the top of the cake. Decorate with violets and leave to set.

LOVER'S KNOTS

Makes 12
25 g/1 oz fresh yeast or 1 tablespoon dried yeast
400 ml/14 fl oz warm water
1 tablespoon sugar
1 × 25 mg vitamin C tablet, crushed
750 g/1½ lb strong plain white flour, plus a little extra
2 teaspoons salt
25 g/1 oz butter
To glaze
beaten egg or milk

If fresh yeast is used, crumble it into a bowl, then gradually add the measured water, mixing until blended. Stir in the sugar and vitamin C. For dried yeast, pour the water into a bowl or jug, sprinkle the yeast on top and stir in the sugar. Leave in a warm place for 10 minutes until frothy, then add the crushed vitamin C tablet.

Put the flour into a mixing bowl with the salt and rub in the butter, then make a well in the centre and stir in the yeast mixture. Mix to a dough with your hands, adding a little more flour if the mixture is too soft, then turn the dough out on to a clean surface and knead for 5 to 10 minutes, or until the dough feels smooth and silky. Divide the dough into 12 equal pieces. Roll each into a sausage about 25 cm/10 inches long, and tie this into a knot. Place the knots well apart on greased baking sheets, cover with oiled polythene, and leave in a warm place until doubled in bulk.

Preheat the oven to hot, 220°C (425°F), Gas Mark 7. Brush the knots with beaten egg or milk to glaze, then bake for 15 to 20 minutes. Cool on a wire rack.

GIFTS FOR LIBRANS

Librans like the elegant, the refined, the perfectly balanced. They have an eye for beauty and they like all pastels, especially pink and soft green. Their flowers are peach and apple blossom, pink and red roses and violets; their gems are diamonds, carnelians and opals and their metal is copper.

Pastels preferred *Colour is important when choosing a gift for a Libran: they tend to favour pastels. An easy, inexpensive gift would be a glass jar of sugared almonds, miniature soaps or cotton-wool balls in pretty colours.*

Exclusive gifts *A Libran, whether male or female, likes almost anything from the beauty counter, the more expensive and exclusive the better! He or she will also like a gift to wear, such as a silk shirt, tie or scarf.*

Bonbons and beverages *Every Libran loves food and would certainly appreciate a luxury gourmet item, particualrly if sweet, or something good to drink: anything from an unusual tea to champagne!*

Paintings and porcelain *You could appeal to a Libran's sense of beauty, selecting a print or painting, piece of porcelain or crystal or an elegant pot plant. Alternatively, choose a gift that reflects the Libran appreciation of culture – a good book, record, theatre token or outing, perhaps.*

CHOCOLATE TRUFFLES

These would make a perfect present for a favourite Libran. For an extra touch of elegance, wrap the truffles in pastel tissue paper and tie with toning ribbons, or pack them into a pretty box lined with delicately coloured tissue paper and trimmed with bows and flowers.

Makes 26-28
225 g/8 oz plain chocolate
50 g/2 oz unsalted butter
50 g/2 oz icing sugar
3 tablespoons double cream
1 tablespoon rum
sifted cocoa, to coat

Break the chocolate into pieces and melt in a bowl set over a saucepan of simmering water, stirring from time to time. Remove from the heat and allow to cool slightly.

In a second bowl, cream the butter with the icing sugar until light and fluffy, then add the melted chocolate, cream and rum. Beat well until all the ingredients are blended and the mixture is light and fluffy. Cool, then chill.

Take teaspoons of the mixture and roll in sifted cocoa to form even-sized balls. Chill until needed, then pack as suggested above.

ROSE PETAL JAM

This luscious jam, made from scented red roses, appeals to the sensual Libran. Be sure to collect petals from roses well away from a busy road. They should not have been sprayed within the last two months.

Makes 1 kg/2 lb
150 g/5 oz scented red rose petals, washed and trimmed
750 ml/1¼ pints water
175 ml/6 fl oz lemon juice
575 g/1¼ lb sugar
5 tablespoons commercial pectin
3 tablespoons triple-distilled rose water

Combine the petals, measured water, lemon juice and sugar in a large saucepan and heat gently until the sugar has dissolved. Bring to the boil, then cover and simmer for 30 minutes.

Add the pectin and rose water, stir well, then boil hard for 5 minutes. Test for a set. To do this, place a teaspoonful of the jam on a chilled saucer. Cool for 20 seconds, then run a finger through it. If it wrinkles at the edges and the sections remain separate, it is ready.

If the jam is not ready, test again in 2 minutes, and keep testing until a set is reached. Cool slightly, then pour into warmed sterilized jars. Cover and seal. Label when cold.

SCORPIO

Scorpio – the 'passionate eater' – is the most determined, secretive, passionate, and mysterious sign of the Zodiac. It belongs to the Water element, is of Fixed quality, is symbolized by the Scorpion and traditionally ruled by Mars, although today it is considered to be at least as much under the rulership of Pluto.

Like those born under the other Water signs, Cancer and Pisces, a Scorpio's instinctive response to life is emotional. They have highly volatile feelings, although they are excellent at concealing them. Scorpios are very private people, preferring to keep their thoughts and feelings to themselves unless they choose to share them. No sign is as intense, powerful or compulsive as Scorpio. People born under this sign never do anything by half measures. Once determined upon a goal, they will set about it with singular dedication, will-power and well-controlled energy. They may not – probably will not – talk much about their ambitions, but will not allow anything to stop them. It is not surprising that Scorpio has the reputation for being a sign which cannot be trifled with! Yet no sign can be more loyal, selfless, brave and truly compassionate to a loved person or cause. Conversely, no sign can be more jealous, cruel, emotional, manipulative or devious.

Light and Dark

Most Scorpios are well aware of their own strengths and weaknesses, of the light and dark of their nature. They often have feelings of insecurity and self-hate, and these can express themselves in feelings of vulnerability, possessiveness and jealousy in relationships. Scorpios need to accept themselves exactly as they are and avoid trying to change themselves, or fight the darker aspects of their nature. As they learn to accept and love themselves, others will find it easier to love them, and they will find that the less pleasant aspects of their nature diminish as they stop resisting them.

Scorpios are as passionate in their relationships as in other areas of their lives. They make extremely loyal friends and generally have one or two really close and trusted friends rather than a large circle. They are also devoted to their families: Scorpios are bound by intense ties of love. They do not, however, mince words and will always tell the blunt truth (unless they are keeping their real feelings hidden for some reason). They also make dreadful enemies; just as there is no more loyal and devoted friend than a Scorpio whose heart has been won, so there is no worse enemy. The Scorpio desire for revenge is strong.

Naturally Psychic

Scorpios often know instinctively what others are thinking and feeling and therefore how to please, hurt or discomfort. They are naturally psychic. Yet if anyone succeeds in discovering one of *their* closely guarded secrets, infringes their privacy, takes them for granted, betrays their trust, or, perhaps worst of all, hurts their pride, a Scorpio will be deeply wounded.

Scorpios follow spare time interests with as much dedication as they pursue any other activity. They frequently have unusual interests such as collecting rare items, studying hypnosis or deep-sea diving. They need an outlet for their intensity, perhaps through some regular form of sport (which they always play to win!) or through an activity such as drama or playing a musical intrument.

Iron Self-discipline

The dedication typical of Scorpio means they are capable of rising to the top in their chosen career if they wish. In fact, thanks to a combination of will-power, single-mindedness and capacity for hard work and iron self-discipline, a Scorpio can achieve any ambition. Never underestimate the power of a Scorpio! They can succeed in many different career fields: numerous actors, actresses, musicians, sportsmen and sports-women can be found under the sign, as well as people eminent in their chosen field. Scorpio is the sign of life and death; of birth, sex, the occult, the hidden and the secret. People born under this sign are often drawn to occupations which involve aspects of these, such as medicine, surgery, nursing, and all fields of science, including research.

Prince Charles has the Sun in Scorpio and his interest in holistic healing, ecology and the more mysterious and hidden side of life is entirely in keeping with his sign and will probably increase as he gets older. If he is a typical Scorpio he will not, however, like people knowing too much about it. Scorpios are extremely secretive and never, ever reveal all that they are thinking and feeling, even to their nearest and dearest!

Foods for Scorpios

Scorpios have keen tastebuds and although they are better able than other signs to discipline themselves regarding food and dieting, they love good food. Many gourmets and connoisseurs of fine wines are born under the sign. Like Aquarians, Scorpios are a law unto themselves. They are also highly opinionated, with strong likes and dislikes which they may express quite vehemently. They often favour unusual food combina-tions. In the matter of food, as elsewhere in their lives, Scorpios are individualistic and mysterious. It is thus not easy to generalize about food likes and dislikes. I have found that Scorpios particularly like cream, and creamy dishes such as mayonnaise. Most enjoy a good home-made coleslaw (with plenty of mayonnaise) and also favour cheese sauce and ice cream.

Scorpios may or may not be vegetarian. I know staunch vegetarians and equally committed meat-eaters born under the sign. But whatever their views happen to be, you can be sure they'll feel passionately about them.

Martian Foods

Garlic bread is another favourite. It is appropriate for the sign, since garlic traditionally belongs to Mars, ruler of Scorpio. On the whole, however, the Scorpios I know are not particularly fond of the other Martian foods, like onions, nettles, horseradish, radishes, rocket, watercress and rhubarb. Basil usually does appeal, as do peppers, which also belong to the sign, although hot chillies and spices are not favoured by the Scorpios I know. Perhaps the natural law of equilibrium means that they are drawn to foods which belong to Venus, the planet which brings the opposite qualities to those of Mars. They like spinach, nectarines, peaches, pears, mint and raisins. Mushrooms, which belong to the Moon, are also popular.

Entertaining, Scorpion-style

Many Scorpios, both men and women, are good cooks. They enjoy entertaining at home, showing off their skills while pleasing their friends. Since they value their privacy highly, an invitation into a Scorpio's home is a compliment and attests to their feelings for you.

When Scorpios entertain, they do so superbly. The table will be exquisitely set and decorated with flowers and candles. The lighting will be subtle and romantic and the mood may be set by soft music. The *pièce de résistance* will be the delectable food, perfectly com-plemented by the wine. This may be dramatic, flam-boyant or surprising in some way, because Scorpios love dishes which supply any or all of these elements. There may be a *soufflé en surprise*; a chilled soup in individual bowls cradled in crushed ice; a bombe for

Dramatic food for intense Scorpios: Kumquats in Brandy (page 99), with pomegranate

dessert or fresh fruit served in a huge ice bowl.

Complicated Dishes

Although Scorpios usually dislike food shopping, they will go to great lengths to get exactly the right ingredients when entertaining. They love a challenge and will attempt complicated dishes so long as the result will be exciting or dramatic enough to justify the hard work. One Scorpio hostess I know made a delectable vegetarian savoury pancake gateau especially for me, consisting of layers of featherlight pancakes and a spinach, ricotta and mozzarella mixture, topped with creamy sauce.

Scorpios and Health

Scorpios are strong in mind and body and can will themselves to get better – or to get ill. Like all the Water signs, they are creatures of mood and subject to feelings of vitality or exhaustion merely as a result of this. Their health can be dramatically affected by the state of their emotions – in particular, their love life. Some activity such as yoga or meditation which brings them inner peace can be very helpful in this respect.

Scorpios sometimes get strange illnesses related to impurities of the blood, and they need a diet rich in fresh fruit and vegetables which are cleansing as well as vitalizing. It is a good idea, too, for Scorpios to drink plenty of pure water.

Body Matters

Parts of the body ruled by Scorpio are the organs of reproduction and elimination; also the lumbar region. Constipation and overweight can both be problems. A sensible diet containing plenty of wholewheat bread, fresh fruit and vegetables may help both conditions. Many Scorpios seem to find some extra high-fibre foods such as bran cereal particularly helpful. In my opinion the problems of constipation and overweight are linked with the Scorpion tendency to eat through frustration or anger, swallowing food along with their feelings, and then hanging on to their feelings for too long. So expressing the emotions through running, swimming or other vigorous exercise, or even through beating a mattress, can help greatly.

The most serious potential danger in a Scorpio's life, however, is not physical injury or disease, but the detrimental effect of the build-up of negative emotions. Scorpios often see a hurt or slight where none was intended and find it difficult to let go of old resentments and grudges. These can make a Scorpio become bitter, and this in turn can affect their health. If they can get into the habit of letting go of people, things and experiences they feel have hurt them, they will feel much lighter, happier and healthier than if they cling on to their wounded feelings, and at the same time, will attract love and good experiences into their lives.

Clockwise from top: Scorpio Nut Loaf; Garlic Mushrooms (page 96); Pears with Tarragon Cream

PEARS WITH TARRAGON CREAM

Although the Scorpios I know are not great fruit eaters, they make an exception for this starter. The combination of the surprise element, the creamy topping and the piquant flavouring always appeals. It is important to choose pears that are really ripe. I find it best to buy them when they are hard, up to a week in advance, and allow them to ripen at room temperature. They should slice easily.

Serves 6
3 large ripe dessert pears, preferably Comice
2 tablespoons lemon juice
12 lettuce leaves
mild paprika
6 tarragon sprigs (optional)
For the tarragon cream
1 × 150 ml/5 fl oz carton double cream
1 tablespoon tarragon vinegar
caster sugar, salt and freshly ground black pepper

First make the tarragon cream. Put the double cream into a bowl with the tarragon vinegar. Add a pinch each of caster sugar and salt and a grinding of black pepper and whisk until the cream is thick but still soft and floppy. Taste the tarragon cream and add a little more sugar, salt and pepper if needed, then chill in the refrigerator until required.

Just before serving, halve and peel the pears. Carefully remove the cores – you will find that a teaspoon is good for doing this. Brush the halved and peeled pears all over with the lemon juice. Put two lettuce leaves on each plate and place a half pear, core-side down, on top of the lettuce.

Spoon the tarragon cream on top of the pears, dividing it equally between them, then sprinkle the tarragon cream with a little paprika and garnish each portion with a fresh tarragon sprig if they are available. Serve the pears at once.

SCORPIO NUT LOAF

This nutloaf makes a delicious main course in a vegetarian meal, and can be served hot with Sherry Gravy and vegetables as suggested below, or cold, with crusty French bread and salads.

Serves 6
25 g/1 oz butter
4 tablespoons dried wholewheat breadcrumbs (ready-prepared bought ones are fine)
2 tablespoons sunflower or olive oil
1 onion, finely chopped
3 celery stalks
3 carrots
100 g/4 oz walnuts
175 g/6 oz wholewheat breadcrumbs
1 × 425 g/15 oz can tomatoes, drained
2 eggs, beaten
1 teaspoon mixed herbs
salt and freshly ground black pepper

Grease a 1 kg/2 lb loaf tin with half the butter, then line the base with a long strip of buttered greaseproof paper or non-stick baking parchment to extend up the sides. Sprinkle with half the crumbs, pressing them into the butter.

Heat the oil in a large saucepan. Add the onion, cover and fry for 10 minutes, stirring occasionally, until lightly browned. Finely chop the celery, carrots and walnuts. Chop the tomatoes or whizz them in a food processor. Add these to the onion, together with the eggs, herbs and seasoning. Spoon the mixture into the tin, level the top, sprinkle with the remaining dried crumbs and dot with the rest of the butter. Bake, uncovered, in a preheated moderate oven, 180°C (350°F), Gas Mark 4 for 1 to 1¼ hours.

Let the nut loaf rest for 3 to 4 minutes before turning out. Serve with Sherry Gravy (recipe follows), roast potatoes, steamed vegetables and redcurrant jelly.

SHERRY GRAVY

750 ml/1¼ pints water
3 teaspoons vegetarian stock powder
3 teaspoons soy sauce
1½ tablespoons redcurrant jelly
1 tablespoon cornflour
1½ tablespoons sherry
1½ tablespoons orange juice

Gently heat the first four ingredients together in a saucepan. Blend the flour, sherry and juice, add a little of the hot liquid, then return all to the pan. Simmer until slightly thickened.

GARLIC MUSHROOMS

According to Culpeper, garlic belongs to Scorpio and is 'a remedy for all diseases and hurts except those which itself breeds . . . is a good preservative and remedy for any plague, sore or foul ulcer; taketh away spots and blemishes in the skin, easeth pains in the ears, ripeneth and breaketh imposthumes and other swellings . . .' With mushrooms it makes a favourite starter for Scorpios. Serve with warm soft bread or rolls.

Serves 4
500 g/1 lb button mushrooms
50 g/2 oz butter or margarine
1-2 large garlic cloves, crushed
salt and freshly ground black pepper

The mushrooms should be roughly the same size, so halve or quarter any large ones. Wipe the mushrooms or wash quickly, then dry on absorbent paper. Reserve until just before serving. Set four deep individual dishes or soup bowls to warm.

Melt the butter in a large saucepan or frying pan. When it is hot but not browned, add the mushrooms and garlic. Stir constantly over the heat for about 3-4 minutes, until the mushrooms are hot and beginning to get tender. Do not let them get to the stage where they produce lots of water. (If this does happen, drain the liquid off and add a bit more butter and garlic).

Spoon the mushrooms into the four bowls and serve.

LINZERTORTE

Warmly spiced, with a sweet/sharp jam filling, this is a delectable pudding.

Serves 6
175 g/6 oz plain wholemeal flour
1 teaspoon cinnamon
a pinch of ground cloves
175 g/6 oz ground almonds
grated rind of 1 lemon
40 g/1½ oz soft brown sugar
175 g/6 oz soft butter
1 egg yolk (optional)
225 g/8 oz raspberry jam
icing sugar to dredge

Combine the flour, cinnamon, cloves, almonds, lemon rind, sugar and butter in a mixing bowl. Add the egg yolk, if used. Mix gently with a fork until a dough is formed. Knead the dough lightly, then wrap in polythene and chill for 30 minutes.

Preheat the oven to moderately hot, 200°C (400°F), Gas Mark 6. Lightly grease a 20 to 23 cm/8 to 9 inch flan dish or loose-bottomed flan tin.

Roll out three quarters of the pastry thickly to fit the dish. Ease into place and trim the edges. Spoon the jam over. Add the trimmings to the remaining pastry. Roll this out, again thickly, and cut into long strips. Arrange these in a lattice on top of the jam. Bake for 25 to 30 minutes, until the tart is golden brown. Dredge with icing sugar. Serve hot, warm or cold.

Above: Linzertorte; below: Tipsy Cake (page 98)

TIPSY CAKE

More of a pudding than a cake, this is delicious, and much loved by Scorpios. It is more alcoholic than it looks, so drivers should be warned.

Makes one 20 cm/8 inch cake
175 g/6 oz self-raising 85% or 100% wholemeal flour
1½ teaspoons baking powder
175 g/6 oz caster sugar
175 g/6 oz polyunsaturated margarine or
softened butter
3 eggs
To finish
120 ml/4 fl oz sherry
100 g/4 oz apricot jam, warmed
200 ml/7 fl oz double cream
15 g/½ oz flaked almonds

Preheat the oven to 160°C (325°F), Gas Mark 3. Grease two 20 cm/8 inch sandwich tins and line the base of each with a circle of greased greaseproof paper.

Sift the flour with the baking powder into a mixing bowl and add the sugar, margarine and eggs. Beat with a wooden spoon for 2 minutes, or in an electric mixer for about 1 minute, until the mixture is smooth, thick and glossy. Spoon the mixture into the prepared tins and level the tops.

Bake, without opening the oven door, for 30 minutes, until the cake layers spring back when lightly touched in the centre. Leave the layers in the tins to cool for 1 minute, then turn them out on to a wire rack and remove the lining paper. Leave the layers to cool.

Stand each layer on a rack over a plate and spoon the sherry over the top. Leave for a few minutes to soak in, then sandwich the layers together with some of the warm apricot jam. Brush the rest of the jam over the top and sides of the cake. Whip the cream and spread all over the cake, then sprinkle with the flaked almonds. Chill for 2 to 3 hours or overnight before serving.

BLACKCURRANT MERINGUE ICE

This sumptuous pudding can be made in advance, frozen, and then used straight from the freezer without thawing. If time is short, use 10 ready-made medium meringue halves.

Serves 6
1 × 350 g/12 oz jar blackcurrants, drained, or 175 g/6 oz
fresh or frozen blackcurrants stewed with 2 tablespoons
water and 50 g/2 oz caster sugar
1-2 tablespoons cassis (optional)
1 × 284 ml/10 fl oz carton whipping cream
2 tablespoons caster sugar
For the meringue
3 egg whites
75 g/3 oz caster sugar

First make the meringues. Whisk the egg whites in a grease-free bowl until stiff, then whisk in half the sugar. When this has been incorporated, fold in the rest. Put spoonfuls of mixture on to a baking sheet lined with a non-stick baking parchment or greased greaseproof paper. Bake in a very cool oven, 110°C (225°F), Gas Mark ¼, for 2 to 3 hours, until dried and crisp. Turn off the heat and leave the meringues to cool in the oven if possible. They will keep in an airtight tin for several days.

While the meringues are cooking, purée the blackcurrants in a blender or food processor, then press the purée through a sieve into a bowl. You should have about 3 tablespoons of smooth purée. Add the cassis to this if you are using it.

Assemble the pudding. In a bowl, whip the cream to soft peaks, then beat in the sugar. Break the meringues into rough pieces, not too small. Fold the meringues gently into the cream, together with the blackcurrant mixture, which should be just rippled through. Put the mixture into a serving dish or polythene container, cover and freeze until needed.

GIFTS FOR SCORPIOS

Scorpios like the dramatic, the unusual, the mysterious, the gift with a surprise element. Their colours are burgundy red, brown and black; their flowers are anemones, gentians and deepest black-red roses; their gems are topaz, malachite, turquoise, ruby, golden quartz and their metal is iron.

Hidden surprises *Scorpios love to feel you have chosen something highly personal to them. Their pleasure is increased if the gift is mysteriously wrapped or even hidden, such as a trinket concealed in a bouquet of flowers.*

Classy and expensive *Luxury and quality appeal to a Scorpio; they enjoy classy, stylish, expensive gifts. A small*

item from a famous designer, a sleek, slim pen, a smart trinket box or a silk tie or scarf would appeal, so would a cashmere sweater or a very special key-ring.

Spicy scents *Expensive scents and bath oil find favour, as do spicy, musky scents. Scented massage oil, herbal skin tonics and luxurious hand cream are good choices.*

Elegant and edible *In the kitchen or dining room, a Scorpio would love any elegant, unusual item such as silver grape scissors, nutcrackers or a cake slice. Edible gifts could include liqueurs, toffee apples, Kumquats in Brandy and raisin slices with a moist, hidden filling (recipes follow).*

KUMQUATS IN BRANDY

Makes 1 kg/2 lb
350 g/12 oz caster sugar
450 ml/¾ pint water
750 g/1½ lb kumquats
about 1500 ml/¼ pint brandy (more if required
– see Method)

Make a light syrup by combining half the sugar in the measured water. Heat gently, stirring until dissolved, then boil for 3 minutes.

Meanwhile, prick the kumquats all over with a darning needle. Add them to the syrup and poach gently for about 5 minutes, or until the kumquats are tender. Remove from the heat and drain the kumquats, reserving the syrup left in the saucepan.

When the kumquats are cool, spoon them into several small jars or into two 500 g/1 lb jars, filling them well. Add the remaining sugar to the reserved syrup in the saucepan and heat gently until dissolved. Bring to the boil and cook until the temperature reaches 110°C/230°F on a sugar thermometer. Allow to cool.

Pour the reserved syrup over the kumquats in the jars so that they are half-filled, then fill to the top with the brandy (you may need to use a little more, so have some extra at hand). Cover and leave for at least 3 months before using.

DATE AND RAISIN SLICES

Makes 12
100 g/4 oz self-raising wholemeal flour
100 g/4 oz rolled oats
100 g/4 oz soft butter or margarine
50 g/2 oz soft brown sugar
For the filling
75 g/3 oz raisins
150 g/5 oz dates
150 ml/¼ pint water
a few drops of pure vanilla essence

Preheat the oven to moderately hot, 190°C (375°F), Gas Mark 5. Line an 18 cm/7 inch square tin with greased greaseproof paper.

Make the filling. Combine the raisins and dates in a small saucepan. Add the measured water and cook, uncovered, over moderate heat for about 15 minutes. Add a few drops of vanilla essence, remove from the heat and leave to cool.

Meanwhile put the flour into a mixing bowl with the oats and butter. Work in the margarine with a fork, to form a crumbly mixture. Stir in the sugar. Press half this mixture into the prepared tin, then put the raisin mixture on top and cover with the remaining flour mixture. Press down well. Bake for 30 minutes. Cut into slices while still warm but remove from the tin when cold.

SAGITTARIUS

Sagittarius – the 'optimistic eater' – is hopeful, jovial and outgoing: it takes a great deal to dampen the spirits of a Sagittarian. This sign is ruled by the planet Jupiter, whose astrological characteristics are expansion, good fortune and optimism. Sagittarius belongs to the warm-hearted, enthusiastic Fire element, along with Aries and Leo, with whom it has much in common.

Sagittarians are active and enthusiastic, entering wholeheartedly into whatever they are doing. They love a challenge or an ideal to aim for and will usually have several equally demanding projects on the go at once. Mini-projects do not excite them; their penchant is for big, far-ranging schemes, enterprises and challenges, and they are much better at starting than finishing.

There is a visionary, idealistic quality about the Sagittarian nature which constantly spurs them on to new interests and activities. They leap into these with a hope and enthusiasm that is heartwarming and courageous. Past failures do not discourage them; if they think about the past at all, their optimism makes them certain this time it's going to be different. If they do hit snags, however, they will accept them with great good spirits and always make the best of the situation. They are wonderful people in a crisis: courageous, inventive and, above all, sure that everything is going to turn out right. Amazingly, this is often the case where Sagittarians are concerned. It is something to do with positive thought and the luck of Jupiter...

Sense of Adventure

Sagittarius is an active, restless sign. One of its keynotes is expansion, and Sagittarians hate feeling restricted, whether mentally, emotionally, or physically. They have a natural sense of adventure and love to travel and explore, their hope and optimism carrying them along and encouraging all their companions, too. This expansiveness affects all areas of their lives. Physically, it often gives a liking, even a passion, for sport or outdoor exercise. Mentally, it means that Sagittarians have active minds and an unquenchable thirst for knowledge, often in philosophical subjects. Emotionally, it gives a warmth and friendliness which embraces everyone they meet, cutting through all barriers of religion, class or creed. Sagittarians appear not to notice such things, but look straight at the real person underneath. They love to exchange a friendly comment, discuss life, their ideas and personal philosophy. The quest for this, is, for many Sagittarians, the most profound interest of all.

In relationships, Sagittarians like to feel they have freedom, as elsewhere in their lives. Yet they are honourable, open and truthful and once happily settled seldom abuse another's trust. The things that hurt them more than anything are when others distrust or deceive them. Fortunately (perhaps because they are so open and honest themselves) they generally get the same treatment from others. Their natural *joie de vivre* enriches their relationships. They are warm and spontaneous, law-abiding and often flirtatious.

Although Sagittarians may appear to be easy-going to the point of unconventionality, they are actually quite traditional; naturally law-abiding except when they think the rules are petty or silly. Big-minded Sagittarians hate mini-bureaucracy and red tape and can be quite rebellious when faced with either of these. Like other Fire signs, Sagittarians have an innate sense of self-worth. They expect others to like them, and this gives them the confidence to talk to anyone from a dustman to a duke as an equal. A more difficult characteristic to cope with is their way of telling you exactly what they think without sparing your feelings, or even realizing they are treading on sensitive and delicate ground. On this account they are not generally renowned for their sensitivity but they are so well-meaning and good natured that fortunately they are usually forgiven!

Diverse Interests

Sagittarians have many interests, and frequently have several on the go at once. These often involve outdoor life, sport or studying and reading deep and often philosophical subjects. This union of the physical with the cerebral is typified by the strange symbol of this sign, which is that of the mythical centaur; half man, half horse.

In the area of work, many Sagittarians are found in careers where they have a natural platform for expressing their ideas, such as teaching, advertising, promotion and public relations. Some become professionally involved with sport or the travel business. They prefer work which gives quick results and is not restricted in its hours – or by red tape, which is guaranteed to arouse ire in a Sagittarian.

Foods for Sagittarians

There may be gourmets born under the sign of Sagittarius, and certainly if the Moon or rising sign are in a food-loving sign like Taurus or Cancer, this is possible. On the whole, however, Sagittarians, like those born under Aries, tend to think of food as fuel, to be grabbed and eaten quickly and heartily to give necessary energy before some more interesting activity is embarked upon.

Sagittarians like good, filling food: plenty of complex carbohydrates like pasta, crusty bread, big jacket potatoes. If the latter have a slightly charred skin from being cooked over a campfire or barbecue, so much the better. Sagittarians often have the Fire-sign liking for crisp, browned foods and slightly burnt flavours and love cooking and eating out of doors – you can always please Sagittarians by inviting them to a barbecue!

Good Plain Cooking

Whether they are cooked indoors or out, Sagittarians like solid square meals. They are not ones for nibbles and dips, and do not care for fiddly garnishes. Plain cooking is their preference, starting, always, with a filling breakfast. My husband is a Sagittarian and will never leave the house in the morning, however early the hour, without breakfast. When Sagittarians are out on hikes or travels, generous sandwiches or filled pittas are generally popular, especially if teamed with sticky parkin or cake. The Sagittarians I know have a particular penchant for thick wedges of bread and honey, steamed syrup pudding, doughnuts, flapjacks, and, best of all, treacle tart (recipe on page 106). They prefer these sweet and solid foods to creamy or airy ones like profiteroles, meringues and soufflés.

Sagittarians do not enjoy routine shopping – 'Routine? what's routine?' – but they love exploring new markets and ethnic shops. There have been many times when I have needed some unusual ingredient for testing a recipe and my husband has always succeeded in tracking it down for me. Sagittarians are willing to try new foods, particularly those from foreign lands, but this is more through a sense of adventure than for gastronomic reasons.

Sage and Sloes

All the foods of Jupiter belong traditionally to Sagittarius. So asparagus, white beetroot, dandelion, samphire, pinenuts and chestnuts are Sagittarian foods. So are bilberries/blueberries, and maple syrup.

Of the herbs, I particularly associate sage with Sagittarius, partly on account of its name, which evokes one of the best aspects of the sign. Purple-flowered

Picnic fare for Sagittarians: Chick-Pea-Filled Pitta Breads (page 106)

borage, chervil, balm, hyssop and sweet cicely also belong to Jupiter and Sagittarius. To introduce the opposite influence to that of Sagittarius and thus help to bring balance, the cooling, calming foods of Saturn are also useful. Sagittarians might therefore like to include red beetroot, barley, sloes and quinces in their diet for their soothing quality.

Entertaining, Sagittarian-style

Sagittarians enjoy social occasions and are warm and hospitable. They are welcoming, generous hosts and hostesses and capable of preparing some delicious feasts for their guests, even though their lack of interest in food means that cooking may be quite low on their list of priorities.

Although Sagittarius is an easy-going sign in many ways, it also has a strange formality, and Sagittarians love the beautifully set table with prettily arranged fresh flowers, gleaming glass and shining silver. When you dine in a Sagittarian's home, you can expect to get first-class treatment plus plenty of warmth, good humour and delicious food.

The food may well be ethnic – a recipe picked up on their travels or charmed out of one of their foreign friends – and there will certainly be plenty of it. Big-minded Sagittarians haven't any patience at all with those people who push small amounts of food fussily around a plate. They invariably like you to eat, enjoy and come back eagerly for more!

Sagittarians and Health

Sagittarians have the vitality and excellent recuperative power common to all the Fire signs, and will burn illnesses off with a short, sharp fever. They also have that most precious asset, unquenchable optimism. This positive attitude inevitably ensures a swift recovery when they do fall ill.

Their interest in sport, combined with a tendency to rush around without looking for pitfalls (this is true both literally and metaphorically), means that people born under this sign are inclined to suffer some bumps, bruises and broken bones.

Vulnerable Spots

The hips, thighs and wrists can be particularly vulnerable areas for Sagittarians, since these are the parts of the body ruled by the sign. Other areas which come under Sagittarius are the liver, arteries and lungs, all of which need care. Sagittarians are right to shy away from creamy, fatty foods and red meat, to keep the arteries clear and the liver functioning well. A diet consisting of plenty of unrefined carbohydrates such as wholewheat bread, oats (often a Sagittarian favourite), pasta, brown rice and fresh fruit and vegetables, together with regular daily exercise and adequate personal freedom will keep a Sagittarian in tip-top health, both physically and emotionally.

Above: Sparkling Wine Cup (page 108); below: Layered Three-Nut Savoury Loaf with Sage and Red Wine Sauce

LAYERED THREE-NUT SAVOURY LOAF

This unusual savoury makes a warming winter main course and is an excellent way of using both pinenuts and chestnuts, which belong to Sagittarius.

Serves 6-8
90 g/3½ oz butter
2 large onions, finely chopped
1 tablespoon wholemeal flour
200 ml/⅓ pint water
1 teaspoon mixed herbs
200 g/7 oz ground almonds, or whole almonds, finely grated
50 g/2 oz pinenuts
100 g/4 oz soft breadcrumbs, white or wholemeal
2 eggs, beaten
salt and freshly ground black pepper
450 g/1 lb chestnuts or 1 × 425 g/14 oz can chestnuts, drained
freshly grated nutmeg

Line a 1 kg/2 lb loaf tin with a strip of non-stick baking parchment long enough to cover the base and extend up the ends. Grease with 15 g/½ oz of the butter.

Heat 50 g/2 oz of the remaining butter in a large saucepan, add the onion, cover and fry for 10 minutes until softened but not browned. Set aside about two tablespoons of the onion. Add the flour to the remaining onion in the pan, stir over the heat, then add the water and stir for 1 to 2 minutes until thickened. Remove from the heat and add the herbs, almonds, half the pinenuts, the breadcrumbs, half the beaten egg and salt and pepper to taste.

If you are using fresh chestnuts, nick the tufted end with a sharp knife, then cook in boiling water for about 10 minutes until the cuts open and the skins will come off with the aid of a sharp knife. Remove all the skins. Place the chestnuts in a small saucepan with water to cover and cook for about 10 minutes until tender. Drain, place in a bowl and mash. If using canned chestnuts, merely drain and mash. Add the remaining onion to the chestnuts, with the remaining 25 g/1 oz butter and egg. Season with salt, pepper and nutmeg.

Put half the almond mixture into the loaf tin. Spread the chestnut mixture evenly on top, then cover with the remaining almond mixture. Sprinkle the reserved pinenuts on the top, pressing them in lightly. Bake the loaf in a preheated moderate oven, 180°C (350°F), Gas Mark 4 for 1¼ to 1½ hours until lightly browned and firm. Carefully remove from the tin. Serve sliced to reveal the different layers.

SAGE AND RED WINE SAUCE

Culpeper says that sage 'is of excellent use to help the memory, warming and quickening the senses'.

Serves 4
300 ml/½ pint water
½ teaspoon vegetarian stock powder
¼ onion, peeled but left in one piece
1 teaspoon dried sage or 1 tablespoon fresh sage
1 bay leaf
300 ml/½ pint red wine
15 g/½ oz butter
15 g/½ oz plain flour
1 teaspoon sugar
a few drops of lemon juice
salt and freshly ground black pepper

Put the measured water, stock powder, onion, sage, bay leaf and wine into a saucepan and boil until reduced by half. Strain into a jug. In a second saucepan, melt the butter and stir in the flour. Heat for a moment or two, then gradually add the strained liquid, stirring all the time. Simmer gently for 10 to 15 minutes to cook the flour. Add sugar, lemon juice and salt and freshly ground black pepper to taste.

ASPARAGUS LATTICE

Serves 6
25 g/1 oz butter or margarine
2 onions, chopped
750 g/1½ lb potatoes, diced
salt and freshly ground black pepper
500 g/1 lb fresh asparagus, washed and trimmed
or 2 × 200 g/7 oz packets frozen asparagus
3-4 tablespoons chopped fresh parsley
2 tablespoons double cream (optional)
For the pastry lattice
175 g/6 oz 85% or 100% wholemeal flour
75 g/3 oz butter or margarine
1-2 tablespoons cold water

Melt the butter in a large saucepan, then add the onions, cover, and fry for 5 minutes without browning. Add the potatoes, season and cover. Cook gently for 10 to 15 minutes until the potatoes are tender but not browned.

Steam or boil the asparagus for about 10 minutes until tender. Drain. Reserve the 6 best asparagus tips; cut the rest into 2.5 cm/1 inch lengths. Add to the potato with the parsley and cream. Mix well. Season, then cool.

Put the flour into a mixing bowl with a little salt. Rub in the butter, then add water to make a dough. Roll out one third of the pastry thinly into a rectangle of 10 × 28 cm/4 × 11 inches. Transfer to a baking sheet or heatproof serving dish. Spoon on the asparagus mixture, leaving about 5 mm/¼ inch clear around the edges. Use the back of the spoon to form the asparagus mixture into a loaf shape. Roll out the remaining pastry thinly and cut it into long strips about 5 mm/¼ inch wide. Criss-cross these over the top and sides of the asparagus mixture. Neaten the edges.

Bake in a preheated moderately hot oven, 200°C (400°F), Gas Mark 6 for 20 to 30 minutes, until the pastry is cooked. During the last 10-15 minutes, wrap the reserved asparagus tips in buttered foil and warm through in the oven. Use to garnish the lattice.

CHICK-PEA-FILLED PITTA BREADS

Serves 4
4 pitta breads
8 large lettuce leaves, shredded
2 tomatoes, sliced
2 carrots, coarsely grated
1 × 425 g/15 oz can chick peas, drained
1 medium avocado, peeled and sliced, or 4 tablespoons mayonnaise (optional)
salt and freshly ground black pepper
½ punnet salad cress

Slit the pitta breads at the top and ease them open to make a pocket for the filling. Fill the pockets with the lettuce, sliced tomato, grated carrot and chick peas. If using avocado, mash and season with salt and pepper, then spoon on top of the other ingredients. Alternatively, top with the mayonnaise. Scatter with cress.

TREACLE TART

Serves 4-5
wholemeal shortcrust pastry made with 175 g/6 oz flour
(see page 141)
100 g/4 oz fine wholewheat breadcrumbs
1 teaspoon lemon juice
350 g/12 oz golden syrup

Roll out the pastry and use to line a 20 cm/8 inch flan dish or pie plate. Trim the edges. Roll the trimmings into strips and set aside. Put the crumbs into the pastry case, avoiding pressing them down, then sprinkle the lemon juice on top. Warm the syrup, then pour over the crumbs. Make sure all the crumbs are covered, but do not mix. Arrange the pastry strips on top in a lattice. Bake in a preheated moderately hot oven, 190°C (375°F), Gas Mark 5 for about 25 minutes, or until lightly browned. Serve warm with custard.

Above: Vanilla Fudge (page 109); Treacle Tart with custard

COFFEE AND WALNUT CAKE

This is a favourite cake with Sagittarians, although one I know prefers it made with skinned and toasted hazelnuts.

Makes one 18 cm/7 inch cake
100 g/4 oz self-raising flour
1 teaspoon baking powder
100 g/4 oz sugar
2 eggs
2 teaspoons good quality instant coffee
7 tablespoons sunflower oil
50 g/2 oz walnut halves
For the filling and topping
100 g/4 oz unsalted butter
275 g/10 oz icing sugar
2½ teaspoons good quality instant coffee
1-2 tablespoons warm water

Preheat the oven to moderate, 160°C (325°F), Gas Mark 3. Grease two 18 cm/7 inch cake tins and line the bases with circles of greased greaseproof paper. Sift the flour, baking powder and sugar into a mixing bowl. In a second bowl, whisk the eggs and add the coffee. Whisk until the coffee has dissolved, then add the oil and mix again. Add this mixture to the flour and sugar and mix well. Reserve 7 of the best walnut halves; chop the rest quite finely and add to the cake mixture. Divide the mixture between the two tins. Bake for 20 minutes, or until the cakes spring back when touched lightly in the centre. Turn the cakes out on to a wire rack and leave to cool.

Make the filling and topping. Place the butter in a bowl and beat in 225 g/8 oz of the icing sugar. In a cup, dissolve 2 teaspoons of the coffee in 2 teaspoons of warm water and mix enough of this mixture into the butter and sugar to make a creamy icing. Spread half the icing on one of the cake layers and place the other on top. Place the remaining icing in a piping bag fitted with a large shell nozzle and pipe whirls of coffee butter-

cream around the top edge of the cake, saving enough buttercream for a final swirl in the centre. Before piping this, cover the top of the cake with coffee glacé icing. Put the remaining icing sugar into a bowl with the rest of the coffee and mix to a pouring consistency with a teaspoon or so of water; pour this over the top of the cake so that it runs to the whirls of butter icing. When the glacé icing has set, pipe the final swirl of buttercream in the centre of the cake, and top with a walnut half. Arrange the rest of the walnut halves evenly around the edge of the cake on top of the buttercream.

SPARKLING WINE CUP

This is an excellent wine cup for a party. If you are serving it in the summer, the finishing touch is a few of Jupiter's flowers, borage, floating on top.

Serves 8
6 lumps of sugar
2 lemons, well-scrubbed
90 g/3½ oz caster sugar
750 ml/1¼ pints water
250 ml/8 fl oz port
250 ml/8 fl oz brandy
a few sprigs of mint or lemon balm
a handful of borage flowers
1 bottle dry sparkling white wine or cider
ice cubes

Rub the lumps of sugar over the lemons. Put the sugar into a large bowl. Cut all the peel and pith from the lemons and slice the flesh thinly, discarding the pips. Add the slices to the bowl with the caster sugar, measured water, port, brandy, mint and borage. Cover the bowl and chill until required. Chill the sparkling wine or cider as well.

When you are ready to serve, add the sparkling wine or cider to the bowl. Serve with ice cubes.

GIFTS FOR SAGITTARIANS

Sagittarians like the unexpected, the witty, the thought-provoking, the foreign, sporty or outdoor, the amusing. Their colours are shades of flame and brown, also deep vivid blue; their plants are fir, dandelions, red roses; their gems are turquoise, carbuncle, jacinth and their metal is tin.

Exotic gifts *Something practical for the outdoor life such as an excellent pocket knife, compass or map-holder might appeal; or a book to remind them of their travels abroad or spur them on to further adventures. They enjoy gifts from exotic places and sporty Sagittarians will welcome anything associated with their own particular passion.*

Book tokens *A Sagittarian with the wide mental interests typical of the sign would love a book on philosophy, travel or religion, or, if you feel unsure of their tastes, give a book token so they can make their own choice.*

Flapjacks or fudge *In the food line, they would enjoy anything to make their time in the kitchen speedy and efficient, ranging from a good can opener to a food processor. And as far as home-made goodies are concerned, a jar of delicious Bilberry Conserve to top their wholewheat door-steps, or some home-made flapjacks or fudge (see below) would be popular.*

BILBERRY OR BLUEBERRY CONSERVE

Culpeper says of bilberries that they are 'under the dominion of Jupiter . . . are good in hot agues, and to cool the heat of the liver. The juice of the berries made into a syrup, or the pulp made into a conserve with sugar, is good for the purposes aforesaid, as also for an old cough, or an ulcer in the lungs, or other diseases therein.' They do make an excellent conserve.

Makes about 2.25 kg/5 lb
1 kg/2 lb bilberries or blueberries, washed and drained
150 ml/¼ pint water
6 tablespoons fresh lemon juice
1 kg/2 lb sugar
250 ml/8 fl oz commercial pectin such as Certo
knob of butter

Put the berries into a saucepan with the water and lemon juice. Bring to the boil, then reduce the heat and simmer without a lid for 10 to 15 minutes or until the fruit is tender. Remove from the heat and add the sugar. Return to the heat, and cook without boiling, stirring until the sugar has dissolved. Then bring to the boil, and boil for 3 minutes.

Remove from the heat and add the pectin, stirring gently, then return the pan to the heat and boil for 1 minute. Remove from the heat again and stir in the butter to disperse the scum.

Allow the mixture to settle for about 5 minutes, then pour into warm, sterilized jars and cover. Label when cold.

VANILLA FUDGE

This delicious but wickedly fattening fudge is an ideal treat for a favourite Sagittarian.

Makes about 575 g/1¼ lb
100 g/4 oz butter
1 × 397 g/14 oz can condensed milk
500 g/1 lb caster sugar
vanilla essence

Line a 20 cm/8 inch square tin with non-stick baking parchment. Put the butter into a large, heavy-bottomed saucepan. Add the milk and sugar and heat gently, stirring until the sugar has dissolved.

Raise the heat and boil for 5 minutes, stirring all the time, until the fudge starts to come away from the sides of the pan and a little dropped into a cup of cold water forms a soft ball. During this time brown specks will rise to the top, gradually dispersing to create a caramel colour. Remove the fudge from the heat, add a few drops of vanilla essence, beat with a wooden spoon until it becomes grainy and begins to set, then pour into the tin. When cool, mark it into squares. Cut into squares when it is completely cold.

CAPRICORN

Capricorn – the 'practical eater' – belongs to the Earth element like Taurus and Virgo, and Capricornians have all the practicality, determination and stability you might expect from this influence. However, Capricorn is also a Cardinal sign, which gives drive and energy, making people born under this sign extremely hard-working and ambitious. They set themselves goals and move steadily and persistently towards them.

Success, achievement and material security are very important to Capricornians; they also have high ideals and standards of perfection. These qualities are embodied in the symbol of Capricorn, the mountain goat, which treads a steady path towards the summit.

Sense of Duty

Saturn, planet of concentration and self-discipline, is the ruler of Capricorn, and these qualities are also evident in the Capricornian personality. The sign gives a strong sense of duty; Capricornians do not take their responsibilities lightly. They are prudent, cautious and conscientious and often worry about fulfilling all their obligations. At the same time, they frequently gravitate to positions of power and take on extra burdens. They like to carry out their undertakings to the letter and they expect others to behave the same way.

In positions of authority they can be rather strict and unbending. Over-rigidity is something which Capricornians need to watch, for it can cramp both their own style and that of others.

It is helpful for Capricornians to cultivate flexibility, warmth and fun; to give themselves permission to enjoy life and not to be always working or worrying. A warm,

lighthearted Capricornian, willing to let her hair down, and able to enjoy the fruits of her labour, is a delight to herself and to others.

Family Pride

Capricorn is the sign of old age, tradition and convention, and most people born under this sign have a particular respect for these. They like the tried and tested and have a sense of family pride; many Capricornians collect antiques or are interested in history and things connected with the past.

In relationships, Capricornians are kind and practical. They are also shy and tend to bottle up their feelings and so may appear rather reserved on the surface. Capricornian control and efficiency can be rather daunting, so that barriers have to be overcome before relationships can develop. Capricornians should have the courage to speak openly about their feelings and not take themselves or others too seriously.

Meeting Challenges

Being hardworking, conscientious, practical, determined and logical, Capricornians can succeed at almost any job they choose. Often, the harder the challenge, the better they respond. Work requiring managerial and business skills is particularly appropriate, also anything connected with building, property or the earth. They enjoy jobs devoted to engineering, history, or which deal with the past and like work that involves planning or economical use of time and effort. Capricornians drawn to the medical world often specialize in work connected with the bones, skin, teeth or the elderly, all of which come under the rulership of this sign.

Foods for Capricornians

Capricornians enjoy food, although they are often quite strict with themselves and may live in a thrifty, spartan fashion. They like simple, traditional dishes, but they also have excellent taste in food and can be discriminating gourmets and connoisseurs of fine wine.

When Capricornians shop for food, they are careful and well-organized. They keep their storecupboard well-stocked so that they can readily rustle up an emergency meal. They will patronize a local family shop, although they also like to shop at an efficient supermarket, especially if they know their way around.

Bulk Buys

They know which products are worth buying in bulk and which are not; which packets offer the best value by weight; and whether foods are really fresh.

Capricornians love traditional food: good, honest dishes, particularly those that remind them of childhood. They are traditionalists and very family-orientated, so celebrations such as Christmas and Easter are particularly important to them.

Honest and Straightforward

All the Capricornians I know prefer simple foods: good bread, meat, potatoes, homely fruit cake, preserves or pies. Foods of Saturn, which have a natural affinity with Capricorn, are barley, medlar, quince, beetroot and sloes. However, in keeping with Culpeper's theory that the antidote to the sign supplies an element that is lacking, I regard the warming foods of Mars, such as onions, leeks, mustard, capers, radishes, horseradish, watercress, basil and hot spices, as excellent for Capricorns. The same applies to the foods of Jupiter. This supplies the opposite qualities to Saturn, encouraging a sense of lightness, fun and *joie de vivre* which counteracts the seriousness of the sign. So, for a more balanced temperament, Capricornians might like to

include asparagus, bilberries, sage, chervil, samphire, pinenuts, maple syrup and chestnuts in their menus.

Entertaining, Capricornian-style

When Capricornians entertain, they do so perfectly, with great attention to detail. Organization is all-important and they will plan the wines carefully to complement the food. Perfectly cooked classic dishes are generally the mainstay of their menus and they take care not to repeat a dish for the same guests. The Capricornian home is welcoming and well-furnished, usually in a classical, traditional way. There may be an emphasis on antiques. The table will be set with best-quality silver, glass and china, with flowers and crisp linen napkins.

Status Symbols

Social entertaining is one of the Capricornian strengths and often an important part of their career strategy. They are conscious of status symbols and have an address book full of people who are well-connected or who could help them to achieve their ambitions. In addition to their ability to entertain handsomely in their own homes, they also know all the fashionable places to eat out. However, once they have found a particularly pleasing restaurant, they prefer to stick to this rather than to experiment with the unknown.

Capricornians and Health

Capricorn is one of the healthiest signs of the Zodiac, even though Capricornian babies and young children can sometimes be a bit weak and in need of extra care. However, once any early problems are overcome, Capricornians keep amazingly well and are renowned among the signs for their longevity. Astrologically, this is due to the strength of Saturn, the ruler of Capricorn and planet of old age. In terms of character it is probably related to the practicality, natural caution and common sense of the sign.

Capricornians are sensible and they seldom take

Honest Capricornian fare: Quince Jelly (page 119) and Mixed Grain Bread (page 118)

risks; they are also amazingly self-disciplined and can be most abstemious in terms of smoking, drinking alcohol and diet. They are also tough and some pride themselves on their hardiness. I know one Capricornian in his eighties who has never worn gloves in the winter, even during the coldest weather, and would consider it a weakness to do so. This same steely quality, plus a natural ambition, causes Capricornians to drive themselves hard, well into old age. This sense of purpose may contribute to their longevity.

Shouldering Burdens

Capricornians are, however, susceptible to some health problems. Their tendency to worry can drag them down, as can excessive overwork and shouldering too many burdens. These may accentuate the Capricornian tendency to take a rather gloomy, depressing view of life. Capricornians can help themselves greatly by cultivating a warm, open and optimistic outlook. Positive thought and creative visualization can be extremely helfpul to Capricornians, as can creating comfort and warmth in their homes, both in terms of temperature and through colour. Warming, soothing foods such as watercress soup, rice pudding or mixed vegetable curry, may also help.

The natural reserve of Capricornians may also affect their health. They benefit from hobbies which give them an opportunity for emotional outlet: acting, public speaking, music – many Capricornians have gifts in these areas – or some other form of artistic expression.

Staying Supple

The parts of the body ruled by Capricorn are the skeletal structure, including the joints and teeth, the skin and gall bladder. These need care. In particular, Capricornians would find it helpful to follow a form of exercise which keeps their joints supple – yoga, perhaps. Rigidity of the body in later life is often a reflection of the state of mind. Capricornians can help themselves here by remaining as tolerant and open-minded as possible and having the courage to try new interests. Nerves and worry can show themselves in skin problems, and often the secret is to address the underlying fear or stress. Once this has been faced and accepted, the rash or eczema often disappears. Capricornians also need to watch their susceptibility to cold; they need to cosset themselves a bit.

With its value to bones, teeth and skin, calcium is an important mineral for Capricornians. They need to make sure that their diet contains adequate amounts of calcium-rich foods such as milk, cheese (including low-fat varieties), yogurt, almonds, sesame and sunflower seeds and broccoli. A vitamin supplement containing vitamin D could be a good idea to ensure the body uses the calcium to the full. A high-fibre diet is also important to combat any tendency to constipation and to keep the gall bladder functioning normally.

Above: Mixed Vegetable Curry with Basmati rice; Cheese and Onion Pie

MIXED VEGETABLE CURRY

Spices from fiery Mars are very good for Capricornians, since they provide an antidote to the coolness and melancholy of Saturn, their ruler. Serve this vegetable curry with boiled Basmati or pilau rice, made according to package directions, or by cooking 225 g/8 oz Basmati rice in 600 ml/1 pint of water with a couple of cloves, peppercorns, ½ teaspoon of turmeric and ½-1 teaspoon of salt. Cook this spiced Basmati rice in a covered saucepan over very gentle heat for 20 minutes until all the liquid is absorbed.

Serves 4
120 ml/4 fl oz oil
1 teaspoon mustard seeds
2 teaspoons turmeric
14 curry leaves, fresh or dried
4 garlic cloves, crushed
5 cm/2 inch length fresh ginger, peeled and grated
¼ teaspoon hot chilli powder
1 cauliflower, broken into florets, to give 750 g/1½ lb
100 g/4 oz whole green beans, topped and tailed
225 g/8 oz carrots, scraped and sliced
8 spinach or cabbage leaves, roughly chopped
salt and freshly ground black pepper
coriander leaves to garnish, if liked

Heat the oil in a large saucepan and add the mustard seeds, turmeric, fresh or dried curry leaves, crushed garlic cloves, grated ginger and chilli powder. Fry the spices for 2 minutes without scorching, then add the cauliflower, beans and carrots. Mix well together, then cook gently until the vegetables are almost tender – this will take about 15 minutes.

Add the chopped spinach or cabbage leaves and cook the curry for a further 5 minutes, until the spinach or cabbage leaves are softened. Season with salt and freshly ground black pepper and serve at once, garnished with coriander leaves, if preferred.

CHEESE AND ONION PIE

This honest, homely pie contains onions and mustard from Mars, plus calcium-rich cheese which is particularly valuable for Capricornians.

Serves 4
225 g/8 oz plain wholemeal flour
½ teaspoon salt
100 g/4 oz butter
3 tablespoons cold water
milk to glaze (optional)
For the filling
3 large onions, sliced
175 g/6 oz grated Cheddar cheese
½ teaspoon prepared mustard
salt and freshly ground black pepper

Preheat the oven to hot, 200°C (425°F), Gas Mark 7. Soften the onions slightly, by cooking them in a saucepan containing boiling salted water to a depth of 2.5 cm/1 inch for 5 minutes.

Drain and leave to cool.

Meanwhile, make the pastry: sift the wholemeal flour into a mixing bowl, adding also the bran from the sieve. Add the salt, then rub in the butter with your fingertips until the mixture resembles fine breadcrumbs. Mix to a dough with the measured cold water, then very carefully roll out half the pastry to fit a 20 to 23 cm/8 to 9 inch pie plate (you may find that wholewheat dough can be a little tricky to handle at first if you are unfamiliar with it – see page 140).

Tip the onions into a bowl, add the cheese and mustard and season to taste. Spoon the onion mixture on top of the pastry. Roll out the remaining pastry to make a lid; press the edges together, trim and make a couple of holes to allow the steam to escape. Re-roll the trimmings and decorate the top of the pie. Brush with a little milk to glaze if liked. Bake the pie for 30 minutes. Serve hot or cold.

STEAMED SYRUP PUDDING

Filling, traditional puddings find favour with Capricornians with their love for hearty, simple food. Here is one of the most popular, made with wholemeal flour for extra nourishment.

Serves 4-6
175 g/6 oz softened butter plus 1 tablespoon
3 tablespoons golden syrup
175 g/6 oz self-raising 85% or 100% wholemeal flour
1½ teaspoons baking powder
175 g/6 oz caster sugar
3 eggs
warmed golden syrup to serve

Fill a steamer with water and heat. Alternatively add sufficient water to a saucepan to come halfway up a 900 ml/1½ pint pudding basin.

Remove the basin and bring the water in the saucepan to the boil.

While the water is coming to the boil, grease the pudding basin thoroughly with 2 tablespoons of the butter, then add the measured golden syrup. Combine the wholemeal flour, baking powder, caster sugar, remaining butter and the eggs in a mixing bowl. Beat these ingredients with a wooden spoon for 2 to 3 minutes until smooth and glossy, then spoon the mixture into the basin on top of the syrup.

Cover the pudding basin with a piece of greaseproof paper pleated in the middle so that it will expand as the pudding rises. Add a piece of aluminium foil, also pleated, and tie securely to the pudding basin with string. Put the basin into the steamer or saucepan of boiling water, cover, reduce the heat slightly and steam the pudding gently for 1½ hours. Do not let the water go off the boil during this time, and keep an eye on the level of the water, topping it up with boiling water if necessary. When the pudding is cooked, invert it on to a plate and serve with extra syrup.

DROP SCONES WITH MAPLE SYRUP

I have included these at the request of one of my favourite Capricornians. Serve them with real maple syrup for a touch of Jupiter's benevolent cheer, or with butter and honey or a preserve – perhaps bilberry – if you want to keep the Jupiter influence.

Makes 24
100 g/4 oz plain 85% or 100% wholemeal flour
pinch of salt
1½ teaspoons cream of tartar
1 teaspoon bicarbonate of soda
2 tablespoons caster sugar
1 egg
150 ml/¼ pint milk
oil or melted butter for greasing

Sift the wholemeal flour into a mixing bowl with the salt, cream of tartar and bicarbonate of soda. Add the caster sugar, then stir in the egg and milk to make a smooth batter.

Grease a large, heavy-bottomed frying pan with oil or melted butter, then place it over moderate heat until a drop of water flicked into it sizzles immediately. Pour 1 tablespoon of the batter into the frying pan to make a drop scone, then repeat several times, spacing the scones in the frying pan so as to allow for spreading. When the undersides are brown and bubbles have risen to the surface, slip the drop scones over on to the other side with a palette knife.

Cook until both sides are golden brown.

Place a clean tea towel on a wire rack. Add the cooked drop scones as you take them from the frying pan, folding the tea towel over them so that they remain soft and moist.

Continue making scones until all the batter has been used, re-greasing the pan between each batch. Serve the drop scones with maple syrup, or with butter and honey or jam.

Clockwise from top: Steamed Syrup Pudding; Drop Scones with Maple Syrup; Rum Butter (page 119)

WHOLEMEAL DUNDEE CAKE

This big, honest, wholesome cake is just right for a Capricornian. It is decorated with their favourite nuts, almonds.

Makes one 20 cm/8 inch round cake
225 g/8 oz butter, plus extra
for greasing
225 g/8 oz soft light brown sugar
4 large eggs, beaten
350 g/12 oz plain wholemeal flour
1-2 tablespoons milk, optional
175 g/6 oz sultanas
175 g/6 oz currants
175 g/6 oz raisins
75 g/3 oz glacé cherries, halved
50 g/2 oz ground almonds
grated rind of 1 orange
75 g/3 oz blanched almonds, split

Preheat the oven to moderate, 160°C (325°F), Gas Mark 3. Grease a 20 cm/8 inch deep springform cake tin with butter and line the tin with a double layer of greased greaseproof paper.

In a mixing bowl cream the butter and sugar until light and fluffy, then add the beaten egg, 1 tablespoon at a time, beating well after each addition. Sift the flour on top of the egg mixture, then fold in gently with a metal tablespoon. Add a little milk if necessary to make a batter which drops heavily from the spoon when you tap it against the rim of the bowl. Gently stir in all the remaining ingredients except for the blanched and split almonds.

Spoon the mixture into the tin, level the surface, and arrange the split almonds on top. Bake for 2½ hours or until a skewer inserted into the centre comes out clean. Cool in the tin for about 30 minutes, remove the cake from the tin, strip off the paper, and leave the cake on a wire rack to cool completely.

MIXED GRAIN BREAD

A mixture of grains makes this a pleasant, substantial, chewy bread, popular with Capricornians and others who like a good, heavy loaf.

Makes one 1 kg/2 lb loaf
1 teaspoon butter
25 g/1 oz fresh yeast or 15 g/½ oz dried yeast and
½ teaspoon sugar
400 ml/14 fl oz tepid water
350 g/12 oz wholemeal flour
175 g/6 oz rye flour
175 g/6 oz medium oatmeal
2 teaspoons salt
1 tablespoon honey
2 tablespoons oil

Using the butter, grease a 1 kg/2 lb loaf tin.

If fresh yeast is used, crumble it into a bowl, then gradually add half the measured water. For dried yeast, pour 200 ml/⅓ pint water into a jug, sprinkle the yeast on top and stir in the sugar. Leave in a warm place for 10 to 15 minutes until frothy.

Combine the flours and oatmeal in a mixing bowl and add the yeast liquid. Dissolve the salt and honey in the remaining water and add to the bowl, together with the oil. Mix to a dough, then turn out and knead on a lightly floured surface for about 5 minutes. Put into an oiled bowl, cover with oiled polythene and leave in a warm place for 45 minutes, or until doubled in bulk.

Knead again briefly, then shape into a loaf and place in the prepared tin. Preheat the oven to hot, 220°C (425°F), Gas Mark 7. Leave the loaf in a warm place for about 20 minutes, or until the mixture reaches the top of the tin. Bake for 10 minutes, then reduce the oven temperature setting to moderately hot, 200°C (400°F), Gas Mark 6, and bake for a further 30 minutes. The base of the loaf should sound hollow when tapped. Cool the loaf on a wire rack.

GIFTS FOR CAPRICORNIANS

The traditional and conventional, the practical, the tried and tested appeal to Capricornians. They like gifts which are useful, either at a practical or intellectual level, and appreciate good design, quality, durability and natural materials. Their colours are the dark shades of brown, green, red and also black. Like Aquarius which also comes under Saturn, their plants are ivy, mosses, heartsease, pansies, holly and amaranthus; their gems are jet, white onyx, moonstone, sapphire and garnet and their metal is lead.

Gourmet treats *If money is no object, foodie Capricornians would enjoy best-quality luxury items, both in food and drink. Less expensive but equally welcome would be goats' cheese, ripe Stilton or matured farmhouse Cheddar, and home-made preserves such as Quince Jelly (see below). Let quality be your guide: if you can only afford an inferior version of a luxury item, it would be better to opt for the best*

quality of something simpler instead.

Natural fibres *If you are buying clothes for a Capricornian, go for traditional styling, natural fibres, muted colours and classy quality – silk, cashmere or finest cotton are the order of the day. Capricornian women like real jewellery in classic settings (for their gems, see opposite).*

Organizers and planners *Capricornians are excellent organizers. Realistic about time, money and resources, they are excellent planners and are able both to delegate tasks and lead others. Any gift that would make use of these skills would be much appreciated, such as a diary, personal organizer, calendar or pocket calculator.*

Music hath charms *Many Capricornians are music lovers, so tickets for a concert, or something for the tape, record or compact disc collection would be welcomed. Make sure you choose the recommended version!*

QUINCE JELLY

Quinces, most delectable of fruits, come under the rulership of Saturn and are thus a fruit of Capricorn. As jelly, they make the perfect gift for a special Capricornian. If you can't get quinces use apples instead, with the addition of some chopped sage, cheering herb of Jupiter; or mint, herb of Venus, for extra flavour and interest.

Makes 1.5-1.75 kg/3-4 lb
1 kg/2 lb firm, ripe quinces
1.5 litres/2½ pints water
about 1.75 kg/4 lb sugar

Cut the quinces into chunks and put them in a saucepan with the measured water. Bring to the boil, reduce the heat and simmer until soft. Strain the liquid through a jelly bag, or colander lined with several thicknesses of cheesecloth, into a bowl; allow to drip without squeezing.

Measure the liquid, return it to the clean pan and add 500 g/1 lb sugar for every 600 ml/1 pint liquid. Bring slowly to

the boil, stirring to dissolve the sugar before the liquid rises in the pan, then boil rapidly until the setting point is reached (see page 141). Skim if necessary, then pour the jam into clean, warm jars. Seal while hot; label when cold.

RUM BUTTER

This is a nice winter-time present for Capricornians to eat with plum pudding or their favourite steamed pudding, or with drop scones. Pack in an attractive pottery jar or serving dish.

Makes about 175 g/6 oz
75 g/3 oz unsalted butter
75 g/3 oz soft brown sugar
2-3 tablespoons rum

In a bowl, cream the butter until pale and soft, then gradually add the sugar, beating well after each addition, to make a light, fluffy mixture. Then add the rum, a little at a time, mixing well to avoid curdling. Spoon the mixture into a small jar or dish, cover with cling film and chill.

AQUARIUS

Quirky, dispassionate Aquarius – the 'unconventional eater' – is an Air sign of Fixed quality. Traditionally it was ruled by Saturn, but since the discovery of Uranus, astrologers have increasingly come to associate this planet with the sign, because the qualities of Uranus – unconventional, dramatic – are in keeping with those of Aquarius. The sign for Aquarius looks like air waves, but the symbol is the man bearing the water pot, which seems odd considering that Aquarius belongs to the Air group of signs, like Gemini and Libra, and not Water.

This contradiction is typical of the sign, and one of many! For instance, Aquarius is the sign of friends and groups, and Aquarians are indeed interested in people and concerned about many social issues. Yet, of all the signs, Aquarius is the most independent: Aquarians need freedom, and have a fear of commitment.

Strong Views

In keeping with the fixed quality of their sign, Aquarians have a great deal of willpower and are extremely determined. They have strong views and fixed opinions, but they consider themselves open-minded (and, indeed, they are, about many things) and also believe in tolerance and personal freedom. They will take advice from their many friends, but will make up their own minds quietly and unaided. Once decided, nothing will sway them. The more outside interference they encounter, the more set they become. Yet they are quite capable of changing course suddenly and for no apparent reason – and then proceeding just as resolutely in the opposite direction. Aquarians enjoy a bit of drama and will sometimes say and do outrageous things just to see how other people will react.

Air of Detachment

The Air element means that Aquarians tend to be intellectual rather than emotional. That's not to say they're not kind, for indeed, they are. They do, however, have a detachment about them and tend to shy away from intense emotional situations. Like all the Air signs Aquarians are inclined to rationalize their feelings and tend to be quite cool, in spite of their friendliness. They love the feeling of isolation combined with closeness that comes from being in a crowd.

Although they have many friends, Aquarians do not find it easy to establish close relationships, with the threat to independence and the need for commitment that they fear this may bring. When a close relationship develops, it usually comes about gradually as the result of a long friendship founded on shared intellectual interests. The chosen partner is usually someone compatible and companionable who brings a feeling of safety because he does not try to bind the Aquarian. Even when an Aquarian has become happily committed to a relationship – and if this happens, it is likely to be a long-lasting one, for Aquarians are very loyal – they need time to be on their own, free as air, thinking their own thoughts. It is important that an Aquarian communicates his or her thoughts and feelings rather than expect partners to pick them up by telepathy.

Interests and Hobbies

It's difficult to generalize about the interests and hobbies of an Aquarian simply because they are so diverse. They generally have an intellectual or social bias and are often concerned with individuals. Aquarians are fascinated by the study of character, so you will find many astrologers, mind-readers and graphologists under this sign, also psychologists, both amateur and professional. They often enjoy acting or being involved with the theatre, or starting new idealistic groups to achieve a particular purpose.

Aquarians are often found in unusual jobs. They are happiest in work in which they can express their originality and individuality. One of the main criteria is that the work appeals to the Aquarian's conscience; this is more important than the pay or prospects. Because of their independent, nonconformist nature, Aquarians tend to change jobs more frequently than some of the other signs. Many Aquarians use their inventive, creative gifts in the field of design or in writing. They may be involved with interviewing or they may be drawn to the technical side of the communications world.

Elusive Charm

Aquarians have a dreamy, idealistic quality which gives them an elusive charm. They often seem to be not quite of this world at all, but more in touch with higher ideas. This is the sign of idealism and dreams and Aquarians can become wrapped up in these, so that they can be vague and forgetful. Aquarians are often years ahead of their time in their thinking and aspirations and may be inspired inventors and leaders, but they are often too independent to form organisations.

Foods for Aquarians

Aquarians are as original, unconventional and unpredictable in their eating habits and prejudices as in every other area of their life. In fact, the only certainty is that their tastes will be unusual. Most Aquarians show their unorthodox likes and dislikes from an early age; the child who insists on eating absolutely everything raw, drinking soup through a straw or mixing pickled beetroot with his ice cream is probably an Aquarian!

Bizarre Diets

We find Aquarians following unusual dietary regimes; I know of one Aquarian whose diet consists practically exclusively of cheese, another who restricts himself to steak and gin, and a third who, after years of struggling with a weight problem, slimmed on the Beverly Hills diet – as bizarre a diet as any Aquarian could wish for – and has remained slim ever since.

Their individuality makes it difficult to generalize about foods for Aquarians. On the whole they love salt, cheese and pickles. One of my zaniest Aquarian friends adores making pickles. It is impossible to walk into her warmly chaotic kitchen without being pressed to try the spicy concoction bubbling away on her stove. Like the other Air signs, Aquarians love dishes which incorporate their element, so a cheese soufflé, meringues and flaky pastry dishes with lots of puffy layers are likely to be particular favourites. I haven't met an Aquarian yet who does not have a penchant for cheesecake and any unusual sweet and savoury mixture, such as damson jam and red kidney beans, or German-style haricot beans in apple sauce. Many Aquarians also love fresh raw vegetables in salads, and plenty of fruit.

Impulse Buyers

Aquarians tend to be impulse buyers and are attracted by products which are new and different. They are moral buyers, refusing, for instance, to purchase any product from a country whose politics they deplore, or which has been involved in any cruelty to animals.

Entertaining, Aquarian-style

If you accept an invitation to dine with an Aquarian, you need to be ready for anything. You might find yourself sitting down to a superb five-course meal; on the other hand, it might be an indoor picnic on folding beach chairs in a bare room, as happened to my husband once.

The food you are likely to be offered in an Aquarian's home will probably be as original as the setting. Perhaps peanut butter or cheese and pickle sandwiches followed

For the cheese-loving Aquarian, Cheddar Cheese and Walnut Spread (page 129)

by cheesecake from the deli, an authentic Mexican or Middle Eastern spread, or hot pancakes straight from the pan in the kitchen.

Sandwiches and Pickles

Cooking does not usually come top of the list of things which an Aquarian likes to do, although sandwiches and pickle-making may be the exceptions! Rebel Aquarians who break this rule bring great flair and originality to their dishes.

An Aquarian's natural instinct is for a clean, ultra-modern kitchen, with plenty of chrome, white, and efficient gadgets. Predictably, though, this is not true for all Aquarians, who need to feel free to put a stamp of individuality on everything in their life, kitchen included. I know many 'perverse' Aquarians who have homely, disorganized kitchens full of books, half-finished crosswords, adopted pets of one kind or another (snuggling up to the warm, ecologically sound, wood-burning fire), collections of art nouveau postcards stuck to the walls, rampant pot plants...

When it comes to eating out, Aquarians enjoy trying new, intriguing places. They love meeting friends at a café or restaurant to reform the world while eating. They are drawn to ethnic restaurants and feel at home in vegetarian eating places run on a communal basis, particularly if associated with some idealistic group.

Aquarians and Health

Aquarians are highly strung and, like the other Air signs, inclined to live on their nerves. They can become so involved in an idea or project that they hardly think of eating, drinking or nurturing themselves, and are inclined to drive themselves relentlessly in pursuit of goals. They can suffer from nervous exhaustion and may become so tense that they find it difficult to sleep.

Individual Effort

Some form of active sport is good for Aquarians; balancing all the mental activity and helping them to relax and establish better sleep patterns. They enjoy exercise in the company of others, especially if it involves individual effort, without competitiveness and teams. Also, they need activities which tone up their systems and help keep the circulation (which can get sluggish) in good working order. Skipping, swimming, cycling, jogging or aerobics would be possibilities. Relaxation and meditation are also useful skills for an Aquarian to learn and use daily.

Aquarius rules the circulation and the lower legs and ankles. Many Aquarians suffer from sprained, swollen or broken ankles or cramps in their lower legs, also piles and varicose veins, and sometimes hardening of the arteries or anaemia in later life. Strengthening the body through sensible exercise helps avoid all this, as does a diet without too much salt or animal fat, and plenty of fresh fruit and vegetables.

Clockwise from top: Mushroom Soufflé Crêpes; Lassi; Chilled Beetroot Soup with Soured Cream (page 126)

LASSI

Yogurt is a food which many Aquarians enjoy, and this light and sustaining Indian drink is ideal for those frequent occasions when they are too busy with friends, projects and plans to think about eating a proper meal or even having a snack. Lassi is sometimes drunk sweet, with the salt replaced by a fruit flavour such as mango.

Serves 1
1 × 150 ml/5 fl oz carton plain yogurt – Greek yogurt is
particularly delicious
75 ml/3 fl oz iced water
salt
powdered cinnamon or cumin seeds
ice cubes

Pour the yogurt into a bowl and whisk it until it is smooth, then gradually add the iced water to it. Flavour the yogurt to taste with a little salt and powdered cinnamon or cumin seeds, and serve in a tall glass with ice cubes.

MUSHROOM SOUFFLÉ CRÊPES

These crêpes have an unusual mushroom filling which incorporates plenty of air, the Aquarian element. Aquarians always love a soufflé, and these 'unconventional eaters' will also like the individuality of this recipe.

Serves 6
100 g/4 oz plain flour
½ teaspoon salt
2 eggs
150 ml/¼ pint milk
150 ml/¼ pint water
2 tablespoons oil or melted butter
butter for frying

For the filling
40 g/1½ oz butter
350 g/12 oz button mushrooms, sliced
1 garlic clove, crushed
50 g/2 oz plain flour
300 ml/½ pint milk
4 eggs, separated
salt and freshly ground black pepper
freshly grated nutmeg
4 tablespoons grated Parmesan cheese

First make the crêpes. This may be done in advance. Either whizz all the batter ingredients in a blender or food processor until combined, or mix the flour and salt in a bowl, break in the eggs and whisk, gradually adding the milk and water, and finally the oil or butter, to make a smooth consistency. Pour into a jug and set aside.

Melt 1 teaspoon of butter in a small frying pan, then pour off the excess, leaving the pan glistening. Pour 2 tablespoons of batter into the pan, swirl the pan so that the batter spreads all over the base, then cook for 1 to 2 minutes, or until set. Flip the crêpe over with a palette knife and cook the second side for a few seconds, then tip the crêpe out on to a plate. Continue in this way until all the batter has been used and you have a pile of 12 to 14 crêpes. Cover and set aside until required.

Preheat the oven to moderately hot, 200°C (400°F), Gas Mark 6. Melt the butter for the filling in a saucepan and fry the mushrooms and garlic lightly for 3 to 4 minutes, until the mushrooms are just tender. Stir in the flour and cook for 1 to 2 minutes. Stir in the milk and cook, stirring, for 2 to 3 minutes until thickened.

Remove from the heat, cool slightly, then stir in the egg yolks with salt, pepper and nutmeg to taste. In a large bowl, whisk the egg whites until stiff, then fold into the mushroom mixture. Heap a little of the mixture on to half of each crêpe and fold the other half over. Arrange the crêpes side by side in a shallow greased ovenproof dish and sprinkle with the Parmesan cheese. Bake for about 20 minutes until puffed up and golden.

CHILLED BEETROOT SOUP WITH SOURED CREAM

Beetroot belongs to Saturn, and therefore to Aquarius and Capricorn. In my experience most Aquarians love it, although, true to the perversity of the sign, I do know of one who claims to loathe it. For the beetroot-loving majority of Aquarians, here is a chilled beetroot soup served with soured cream and chives. This deep red, sweet-tasting soup is delicious accompanied by hunks of warm soda bread.

Serves 6
1 tablespoon oil
1 onion, chopped
225 g/8 oz potatoes, diced
500 g/1 lb cooked beetroot, peeled and diced
1.2 litres/2 pints vegetable stock or water
grated rind of 1 lemon
1 tablespoon lemon juice
salt and freshly ground black pepper
For the topping
1 × 150 ml/5 fl oz carton soured cream
chopped chives

Heat the oil in a large saucepan and fry the onion, covered, for 5 minutes without browning. Add the potatoes, cover the pan again and cook gently for a further 5 to 10 minutes. Add the beetroot and stock or water. Bring to the boil, reduce the heat, cover and simmer the soup for about 20 minutes until the potatoes are tender.

Purée the beetroot soup in a blender or food processor, then add the lemon rind and lemon juice, with salt and freshly ground pepper to taste. Allow the soup to cool, then pour it into a bowl, cover and chill in the refrigerator until ice-cold.

Serve the soup in chilled bowls, topping each portion with a spoonful of soured cream and a scattering of chopped chives.

BAKED ALASKA

This, to me, expresses the Aquarian nature perfectly, with its rather bizarre, surprise element, its contrast of ice and heat, and its topping of airy meringue.

Serves 4-6
For the sponge base
50 g/2 oz soft butter or margarine
50 g/2 oz caster sugar
50 g/2 oz self-raising flour
1 egg
grated rind of ½ lemon
For the filling
1 small ripe pineapple, chopped or 1 × 350 g/12 oz can pineapple in natural juice, drained
1 × 1 litre/1¾ pint block of vanilla ice cream
For the topping
2 egg whites
100 g/4 oz caster sugar

Make the sponge base. Preheat the oven to moderate, 180°C (350°F), Gas Mark 4. Combine all the ingredients in a mixing bowl and beat together for 2 to 3 minutes until smooth, light and glossy. Spoon this mixture into a lightly greased 20 cm/8 inch flan dish or shallow oval dish. Bake for 20 minutes, until the sponge is risen and cooked through. Allow to cool in the dish.

Raise the oven temperature to hot, 220°C (425°F), Gas Mark 7. Arrange the pineapple on top of the sponge in an even layer, leaving the edges clear. Shape the ice cream as necessary so that it fits on top of the pineapple, mounding it up into a dome.

Make the topping. In a medium bowl, whisk the egg whites until stiff, then whisk in half the sugar. Fold in the remaining sugar. Spread this meringue mixture on top of the ice cream, taking it right to the edges of the dish and making sure it covers the ice cream completely. Bake for 5 minutes, until the meringue begins to become crisp on top. Serve immediately.

Above: Baked Alaska; below: Aquarian Cheesecake (page 128)

AQUARIAN CHEESECAKE

All the Aquarians I know love cheesecake and this one is particularly deep and luscious. Top it with strawberries or black cherries in summer, green and purple grapes in winter.

Serves 8
100 g/4 oz digestive biscuits
50 g/2 oz butter, melted
For the filling
3 large eggs, separated
100 g/4 oz caster sugar
500 g/1 lb curd cheese
25 g/1 oz cornflour
grated rind of ½ lemon
1 × 150 ml/5 fl oz carton soured cream
For the topping
225 g/8 oz strawberries, black cherries or black and green grapes
4 tablespoons melted redcurrant jelly or, for the grapes, clear honey

Preheat the oven to moderate, 160°C (325°F), Gas Mark 3. Crush the biscuits with a rolling pin, then mix with the melted butter. Press this mixture into the base of a greased 20 cm/8 inch springform tin.

In a large bowl, whisk the egg whites until stiff; set aside. In a second bowl, whisk the yolks with the sugar until thick and light, then stir in the curd cheese, cornflour, grated lemon rind and soured cream. Fold the whites into the mixture, then pour the mixture into the biscuit crust.

Bake for 50 to 60 minutes, or until set. Switch off the heat and leave the cheesecake to cool in the oven. To finish the cheesecake, hull and halve the strawberries or grapes, removing the pips; remove the stones from the cherries. Arrange the fruit on top of the cheesecake, then brush the melted redcurrant jelly or honey over the top to glaze.

TOMATO SOUP CAKE

This cake illustrates the unusual and enterprising use of ingredients that is typical of this sign. My father, who is a true-blue Aquarian if ever I knew one, used to make it when my sister and I were young, and he has given me his tried and tested recipe for this book. It is surprisingly good, but it is better not to tell people what is in it until after they have eaten it, unless they are ever-unconventional Aquarians who will be willing to give it a try!

Makes one 1 kg/2 lb cake
225 g/8 oz plain wholemeal flour
2 teaspoons baking powder
1 teaspoon cinnamon
1 teaspoon grated nutmeg
½ teaspoon salt
1 teaspoon baking powder
100 g/4 oz butter or margarine
175 g/6 oz soft brown sugar
1 teaspoon bicarbonate of soda
1 × 298 g/10½ oz can condensed tomato soup
90 g/3½ oz raisins
90 g/3½ oz chopped nuts

Preheat the oven to moderate, 180°C (350°F), Gas Mark 4. Line a 1 kg/2 lb loaf tin with greased greaseproof paper. Sift the flour, baking powder, cinnamon, nutmeg and salt on to a plate or piece of greaseproof paper and leave on one side.

Put the butter into a mixing bowl with the sugar and beat until light and pale. Set aside. Add the bicarbonate of soda to the soup in a saucepan. Heat, stirring until dissolved, then add this mixture to the creamed fat and sugar and mix well. Fold in the sifted flour mixture, and the raisins and nuts. Turn the mixture into the prepared tin and bake for 1½ hours, or until a skewer inserted into the centre comes out clean. Invert the cake on to a wire rack to cool.

GIFTS FOR AQUARIANS

Aquarians like the unusual, the surprising, the modern and the bizarre, and are unconventional and original in their tastes. Their colours are shades of electric blue, turquoise, shocking pink – unusual, iridescent shades. Their plants are mosses, ivy, pansies and heartsease, amaranthus, holly; their gems are opal, sapphire, chalcedony and their metal is lead.

Pots of fun *Aquarius is not a 'foodie' sign – being much more interested in people, conversation and ideas, Aquarians do not usually put food and drink high on their list of priorities. Although very individualistic in their tastes in food, most would welcome a home-made pickle or a cheese dip in an attractive pottery pot – preferably hand-thrown and ethnic in origin.*

Dress sense *Aquarians like unusual, striking clothes and jewellery and would be delighted with something to wear. If you know their taste well, do chance this. A street market or ethnic shop would be a better hunting ground than a designer store. If the recipient of your gift wears jewellery it is most likely to be chunky tribal-style or of excellent, clean modern design.*

Looking and listening *An unusual painting, print or ornament would delight an Aquarian, as would a photograph album, original writing materials or something for the stereo collection. With their fascination for the world of thought and theory, Aquarians would also appreciate any books or materials on astrology, philosophy or psychology, or similar mind-stretching topics. Unless they have a very serious nature and are heavily into ecology, small amusing gadgets might also prove popular, as might some electronic 'toy' (Aquarius love high-tech).*

CELERY AND TOMATO RELISH

Aquarians usually enjoy cheese with pickles or relishes, and this easy sweet and sour relish makes a good present for a favourite Aquarian.

Makes about 1 kg/2 lb

2 large heads of celery (outer sticks only), diced
500 g/1 lb tomatoes, cored, skinned and chopped
1 red pepper, seeded and chopped
100 g/4 oz soft brown sugar
2 teaspoons salt
½ teaspoon mustard powder
¼ teaspoon each of ground cloves, allspice, cinnamon and celery seeds
2 teaspoons white mustard seeds
300 ml/½ pint white wine vinegar

Combine all the ingredients in a large saucepan and bring to the boil. Reduce the heat and simmer gently for about 1 hour, until the mixture has thickened. Spoon into clear sterilized jars and label when cold.

CHEDDAR CHEESE AND WALNUT SPREAD

This may be served as a first course, with the crisp, salty biscuits Aquarians love, or as part of a light snack meal, with *crudités* and salad. Packed into an attractive pottery dish, it also makes a good gift.

Makes 300 ml/½ pint

225 g/8 oz mature Cheddar cheese, grated
50 g/2 oz soft butter
50 g/2 oz chopped walnuts
pinch of cayenne
3 tablespoons brandy
To finish
1 walnut half
cayenne

Combine all the ingredients in a bowl and mix well. Spoon the mixture into an attractive dish and level. Press the walnut half into the top, dust with cayenne pepper and refrigerate until required.

P I S C E S

Pisces – the 'dreamy eater' – is sensitive, restless, changeable and imaginative. It belongs, like Cancer and Scorpio, to the Water element; is of Mutable quality, ruled by Jupiter and Neptune, and symbolized by two fish swimming in opposite directions.

The Water element can be seen in the natural Piscean response to life, which is emotional. They are very sensitive to the atmosphere around them and sense the thoughts, needs and feelings of others. Just as water is moulded by the shape of the container that holds it, Pisceans take on the character, mood or atmosphere of their surroundings, and the personalities of those around them. For this reason, coupled with the fact that their own moods fluctuate constantly, Pisceans can sometimes get quite confused about their identity!

Caring for Others

Pisceans are kind, caring people. They are inclined to adapt themselves to others and overlook their own needs. This means they can get the feeling that they are constantly doing things for others and that there is no one there for them. One of the principles of the sign is sacrifice, also surrender and martyrdom, but there is no need for a Piscean to go this far!

It is very important for Pisceans to think about themselves and what they really want and to give themselves the same love and care they would give others. Sometimes they do not even have a clear idea of their own wishes, so accustomed are they to sublimating these. This can lead to sadness, resentment and bitterness; also dependency on loved ones, whom the Piscean tends to cling to and manipulate emotionally in subtle ways. Pisceans must take notice of their own needs, and make sure these are fulfilled, not by expecting others to sense their thoughts and feelings but by stating clearly what their wishes are. Learning to say 'no' to others sometimes is also important. A good book on assertiveness could be very helpful.

Masses of Charm

Pisceans are clever, creative, imaginative people. They have masses of charm and could succeed in many spheres, particularly those involving artistic expression, sensitive handling of people, or the stage. The problem is that many Pisceans, owing to the Mutable quality of the sign, are restless and tend to drift. They do not find it easy to be practical (unless they have a good balance of the Earth signs in their horoscope or a strong influence from disciplined Saturn). This means they often fail to make the most of their ideas and talents.

Pisceans are dreamy, easy-going, indecisive and sometimes too sensitive to face up to the harsh realities of the world. They may be inclined to live in a world of fantasy, instead of getting to grips with reality.

They tend to be unconventional, often seeming to slither out of rules and regulations through a combination of charm and turning a blind eye. When problems come along, they often manage by ignoring them. When I asked my Piscean daughter Katy how she was coping with a particularly stressful situation, she said: 'I just switch off and let the difficulties drift over me.' The real test for a Piscean is to face life as it really is, without illusion and self-deception. Accepting that difficulties and tears exist is vital, rather than repressing them so that they become fears in the unconscious which can cause greater problems. The Piscean who accepts this truth can become open to the spiritual world beyond the physical; to the influence of Neptune, the mystical planet. Great poets, mystics, artists and visionaries can be thus inspired.

Foods for Pisceans

Easy-going Pisceans like most foods. They tend to eat a particular food if it is there, but don't bother much if it is not. They like the idea of pure foods and use some wholefoods, but are not likely to be fanatical about this, or indeed about anything else, unless there are other aspects to the horoscope, such as a strong Sagittarian or Capricornian influence. Some Pisceans (including Katy) are vegetarian out of a natural compassion and love for animals; others are too easy-going to make a definite decision about this, but most are not keen on red meat.

Foods which traditionally belong to Pisces are all types of seafood; asparagus and bilberries (useful for this fluid-retaining sign because of their natural diuretic properties); chestnuts, pinenuts; maple syrup; samphire and white beet. Herbs include borage, sage, balm, chervil and sweet cicely. None of these foods, apart from pinenuts – and chestnuts when bought freshly roasted from the chestnut man on a chilly winter's night, or roasted in front of a flickering fire – is particularly popular with the Pisceans I know. They tend to prefer the ingredients which come under the Sun, Moon and Venus, perhaps naturally seeking to balance the Jupiter quality of their own nature with complementary influences. They love citrus fruits and the lemony flavourings of the Sun; the melons and cottage cheese of the Moon; tomatoes, from Venus, especially when grilled or made into a soothing soup, and celery from Mercury.

Melon and Madeira Cake

Very strongly flavoured foods such as ripe Stilton, chilli or curry do not appeal, but most seafood is generally popular, as are gentle foods like melon and Madeira Cake (see page 138). Katy loves these and also enjoys mashed potatoes, plain rich tea biscuits, oatcakes, anything flavoured with almonds, either sweet, such as macaroons, or made into a savoury, such as the Crunchy Almond Slices (see page 135). She also likes almonds blanched and added to a stir-fry. Profiteroles and Crêpes Suzette (see pages 136 & 138) are her favourite puddings. Katy likes cheesecake and trifle, but is not keen on very cold foods, like ice cream. Both she, and another Piscean friend, also seem to drink a lot of pure fruit juice, and tea, and her favourite alcoholic drink is Martini and lemonade. She does not like to eat hot food with cold – my habit of serving a salad automatically with everything is not popular with her and she doesn't much care for vinaigrette. She prefers a fruit-based salad, such as the Florida Salad (see page 135), to my green ones. She, in common with other Pisceans, prefers food served quite simply, perhaps with a delicate sauce.

Shopping for food with a Piscean is a very different experience from shopping with a member of the opposite sign, tidy, well-organized Virgo. I speak from experience, because with a daughter born under each sign, I've frequently done both! The Virgo, Meg, will have a neat list, written in correct order for the supermarket aisles. She knows all the best buys and which brands are to be avoided because of sneaky additives. She shops with quiet efficiency and sorts her items into categories as she packs them. On the other hand, the Piscean, Katy, will drift along as if in a daze, taking things off the shelves as if led by some psychic guidance. She will probably overestimate quantities, miss her place in the check-out queue, then bundle all the items into boxes and bags as quickly as possible and beat a hasty retreat. When a Piscean gets the shopping home, it is likely to be to a homely kitchen, not overly tidy, a comforting refuge for friends with problems as well as the odd stray animal which the kind-hearted Piscean has adopted.

Entertaining, Piscean-style

At heart Pisceans are deeply private people; indeed,

*A special treat for a favourite Geminian: Brandy
Snaps filled with cream (page 139)*

caring, most Pisceans can cook well, although they seldom bother if it's just for themselves. For a special occasion, the colours, flavours and textures will be carefully coordinated, and there will be artistic and tasteful garnishes.

Pisceans and Health

A Piscean's state of health is affected by his or her mood – which changes constantly – and the prevailing atmosphere. Some can also be surprisingly susceptible to certain foods or conditions which may cause strange, allergic reactions. A change of environment can sometimes bring on a cold for sensitive Pisceans; they are also inclined to fungal complaints, particularly athlete's foot. Indeed, their feet are one of their most sensitive areas, and if they get their feet wet, this can all too frequently lead to a cold.

Fluid retention is another problem which Pisceans can encounter. Flushing the system out with plenty of pure water – at least eight glasses a day – and taking some of the diuretic foods, such as steamed asparagus or bilberries, or diuretic drinks such as dandelion coffee or tea, may help.

Bottled-up Feelings

One of the factors which can have a major bearing on a Piscean's health is the state of the emotions. Expressing their feelings and making sure their needs are met as described previously can make a great deal of difference. Bottled-up emotions lead to a feeling of deadness and can eventually result in illness. Sometimes Pisceans suppress their feelings through alcohol or drug abuse, overeating or excessive consumption of caffeine. It is a sign which gives an addictive nature and to prevent habituations forming it is important to locate the emotional problem.

Pisceans do not take to vigorous exercise generally, though like Cancerians they enjoy swimming and dancing or exercising to music and also walking in the countryside.

retirement and seclusion are aspects of life which come under the sign. So however sociable a Piscean is – and they can be very welcoming and inviting – they always, like all the Water signs, keep something of themselves hidden. They need periods of solitude and value time spent on their own.

When a Piscean invites you to a meal, however, you may be sure that it will be a delightful experience. In particular, Pisceans are brilliant at creating mood and atmosphere. Their home is likely to be decorated in soft, harmonizing colours, and there may be some particularly attractively arranged drapes. For the occasion they will enhance the naturally gentle, romantic setting with fresh flowers, candles, subtle lighting and soft music.

Memorable Meals

The food will be delicious. Imaginative, sensitive and

Clockwise from top: Florida Salad; Crunchy Almond Slices; Chilled Two-Colour Melon Soup

FLORIDA SALAD

This salad is as easy on the eye as it is on the palate. Decorate it with purple borage flowers, if possible. These flowers of Jupiter are harmonious to Pisces. According to Culpeper they 'comfort the heart of those that are in a consumption, or troubled with often swoonings, or passions of the heart'.

Serves 2
1 grapefruit
1 orange
1 apple
225 g/8 oz black grapes
a few leaves of oak leaf lettuce
225 g/8 oz cottage cheese

Peel the grapefruit and orange with a sharp knife, cutting away the skin and white flesh altogether, then cutting the segments away from the inner skin. Hold the fruit over a bowl as you work to catch the juice.

Slice the apple thinly into the bowl, removing the core, then halve the grapes and remove the seeds.

Arrange a few lettuce leaves on each plate, then spoon the cottage cheese on top. Arrange the fruits attractively around the cheese and serve at once.

CHILLED TWO-COLOUR MELON SOUP

Pisces, with its two fish, is one of the dual signs, along with Gemini and Sagittarius. This soup made from melons of contrasting colours, emphasizes this quality.

Serves 8
1-2 Ogen melons, total weight about 1.25 kg/2½ lb
1-2 Charentais melons, total weight about 1.25 kg/2½ lb
2 tablespoons caster sugar
8 sprigs of fresh mint

Cut each melon in half and remove the seeds. Scoop out the flesh, keeping the colours separate. Purée the Ogen melon in a blender or food processor and sweeten with half the sugar. Pour into a large jug and chill. Repeat the process with the Charentais melon.

To create the two-colour effect, as in the photograph, position a jug on either side of a bowl and pour simultaneously so that each half of the bowl holds a different colour. Fill all the bowls in the same way and decorate each with a sprig of mint.

CRUNCHY ALMOND SLICES

These crunchy almond slices make a pleasant vegetarian main course. Serve them with a creamy vegetable or hot composite vegetable dish.

Serves 4
2 teaspoons butter
100 g/4 oz Weetabix, crumbled
100 g/4 oz ground almonds, or finely grated nuts
100 g/4 oz margarine
50 g/2 oz flaked almonds
50 g/2 oz pinenuts
1 garlic clove, crushed
2 tablespoons very finely grated onion
½ teaspoon mixed herbs
salt and freshly ground black pepper

Grease a 28 × 23 cm/11 × 9 inch Swiss roll tin with the butter. Put the crumbled Weetabix into a bowl with the ground almonds and rub in the margarine, as if for pastry, until the mixture resembles fine crumbs.

Add the flaked almonds, pinenuts, garlic, onion and mixed herbs. Season with salt and pepper. Press the mixture firmly into the tin.

Bake in a preheated hot oven, 230°C (450°F), Gas Mark 8 for 15 to 17 minutes or until browned and crisp. Cut into triangles and serve hot or cold.

CELERY IN CREAM WITH PINENUTS

Tender celery in a delicate creamy sauce with a sprinkling of Jupiter's nut, the pinenut, makes just the sort of soothing dish that Pisceans like. This may be served in individual dishes as a starter. For a special vegetable dish or for a vegetarian main course, add creamy mashed potatoes and something colourful to please the eye – peperonata (sweet pepper and tomato casserole) perhaps, or grilled tomatoes.

Serves 4-6
4 celery hearts or 2 large heads of celery
salt and freshly ground black pepper
freshly grated nutmeg
1 × 142 ml/5 fl oz carton double cream
50 g/2 oz pinenuts

Wash the whole heads of celery under cold water, then cut the hearts downwards into halves or quarters. If using two large heads, cut off the hearts to a length of about 15 cm/6 inches, then cut them into quarters. Cut the remaining pieces of celery into pieces of about 5 cm/2 inches in length.

Put the celery into a large saucepan. Add enough cold water to come halfway up the celery, sprinkle with a little salt, then bring to the boil. Reduce the heat, cover and simmer for about 30 minutes or until the celery is very tender. (This may alternatively be done in a pressure-cooker, in which case it takes 10 minutes on High Pressure.)

Drain the celery well, reserving the stock for use in another recipe. Place the celery in a shallow ovenproof dish or divide between 4 to 6 individual dishes. Season with freshly ground black pepper and grated nutmeg, then pour the double cream evenly over the top. Sprinkle evenly with the pinenuts. Bake the celery, uncovered, in a preheated moderately hot oven, 200°C (400°F), Gas Mark 6, for about 30 minutes, or until the pinenuts are lightly browned.

PROFITEROLES

Another all-time Piscean favourite, these may be made with wholemeal or white flour.

Serves 6
50 g/2 oz butter or block margarine
150 ml/¼ pint water
65 g/2½ oz plain or strong flour
2 eggs, lightly beaten
For the filling and topping
100 g/4 oz plain chocolate, broken into pieces
1 × 142 ml/5 fl oz carton single cream
1 × 284 ml/10 fl oz carton whipping cream

Preheat the oven to moderately hot, 200°C (400°F), Gas Mark 6. Combine the fat and water in a saucepan. Heat gently until the fat melts, then bring to the boil. Remove from the heat and add the flour all at once, beating well with a wooden spoon. Return to the heat and stir for 1 minute until the dough leaves the side of the pan.

Remove the pan from the heat and tip the dough into a clean bowl. Add about a quarter of the egg, beating vigorously until the dough has absorbed the egg and become glossy again, then add another quarter and beat again. Continue until sufficient of the egg has been absorbed to create a mixture that is glossy and soft but not sloppy. If you choose to use wholemeal flour, you will only require about three quarters of the egg.

Pipe or spoon rounded teaspoons of the mixture on to an ungreased baking sheet, 5 cm/2 inches apart. Bake for 30 minutes. Pierce each puff with a knife to release the steam, then transfer to a wire rack to cool.

Just before serving the profiteroles, make the chocolate sauce. Put the chocolate pieces into a small saucepan with the cream. Heat gently until the chocolate melts. Stir and remove from the heat. Fill the profiteroles with whipped cream, using a piping bag or spoon. Put on individual plates, or pile in a pyramid on a serving dish, and pour the sauce over the top.

Above: Madeira Cake (page 138); below: Profiteroles

CRÊPES SUZETTE

Pisceans like almost any crêpes but Crêpes Suzette, with their delicate citrus flavouring, are top favourite.

Serves 4
100 g/4 oz wholemeal flour
½ teaspoon salt
2 eggs
300 ml/½ pint milk and water mixed
1-2 tablespoons melted butter or flavourless cooking oil
oil or melted butter for frying
For the sauce
100 g/4 oz butter
150 g/5 oz caster sugar
grated rind and juice of 3 medium oranges
grated rind and juice of 1 lemon
4 tablespoons brandy

First make the crêpes. Put all the ingredients into a blender or food processor and blend until smooth. Alternatively, put the flour and salt into a bowl, mix in the eggs, then gradually beat in the milk mixture and melted butter. Brush the inside of a small frying pan with oil or melted butter. Set the pan over a high heat until a drop of water flicked into it sizzles immediately.

Remove the pan from the heat and pour in 1½ to 2 tablespoons of batter for thin crêpes (more for thick ones), tipping the frying pan as you do so, so that the batter runs all over the base. Immediately return the pan to the heat. Cook the crêpe for about 30 seconds, until it is set on top and golden brown underneath, then flip it over, using your fingers and a small palette knife, and cook the other side. Stack on a plate and keep warm. Regrease the frying pan as necessary.

To make the sauce, melt the butter, sugar, orange rind and juice and lemon rind and juice in a shallow flameproof casserole. When all the sugar and butter has melted, remove from the heat. Dip a crêpe in the mixture on both sides, folding it in half and then in half

again to make a triangle, then push to the side of the casserole. Repeat until all the crêpes have been used, leaving them in the casserole.

Just before serving, heat the crêpes gently, then raise the heat to high for 1 minute so that the sauce becomes really hot. Pour in the brandy and set alight with a taper or by tipping the casserole down towards the gas flame. Transfer carefully to the table. The flames will die down in a few seconds.

MADEIRA CAKE

The delicate flavour and texture of this cake make it a favourite with Pisceans.

Makes one 20 cm/8 inch round cake
175 g/6 oz unbleached plain flour
175 g/6 oz self-raising flour
250 g/9 oz butter
250 g/9 oz vanilla sugar or caster sugar with 1½
teaspoons vanilla essence
4 large eggs, beaten
2-3 tablespoons milk (optional)
2-3 thin slices citron peel

Preheat the oven to moderate 180°C (350°F), Gas Mark 4. Grease and line a 20 cm/8 inch round cake tin with greased greaseproof paper. Sift the flours together on to a piece of greaseproof paper. In a mixing bowl, cream the butter and sugar until light, pale and fluffy, then add the beaten egg, a little at a time, beating well after each addition. Add the vanilla essence, if using, then fold in the flours, adding a little milk if necessary to make a soft, dropping consistency. Spoon the mixture into the tin, and level the top.

Bake for 20 minutes. Lay the citron peel on top of the cake and continue to bake it for a further 40 minutes, or until a warmed skewer inserted into the centre comes out clean. Turn out on to a wire rack and cool.

GIFTS FOR PISCEANS

The dreamy, the soft, the romantic and the idealistic appeal to Pisceans – they love gifts which take them out of themselves. Their colours are white and sea colours such as shades of purple, grey, and blue; their flowers are traditionally red roses although almost any flowers would appeal to sentimental Pisceans; their gems are amethyst, chrysolite and topaz and their metal is tin.

Books for bookmen *Pisceans love to lose themselves in books. Choose a good novel, if you know their taste. Alternatively, an anthology of poems or collection of photographs would prove popular, or a study on philosophy.*

Natural objects *An artistic gift, such as a painting, print or photograph in a fine frame would go down well. So would scented candles or a pretty vase. Look to the sea for inspiration – perhaps natural objects such as shells or even a piece of attractively shaped bleached driftwood. Dried flowers or pot-pourri would be other possibilities.*

Food thoughts *In the kitchen they like gifts made from materials such as wood or terracotta. Small gadgets for decorating food for special occasions often appeal – cocktail cutters, a piping set or an orange zester. Edible gifts they would enjoy include quality tea, Brandy Snaps (see below), oatcakes and Roquefort Dip (see below), or a pot of their herbs (sage, balm, borage or chervil).*

BRANDY SNAPS

A present to indulge a favourite Piscean. Fill the brandy snaps with cream just before you give them or simply pack them in a tin, with or without a carton of cream as a bonus.

Makes 20
50 g/2 oz butter
100 g/4 oz caster sugar
50 g/2 oz golden syrup
50 g/2 oz plain 85% wholemeal flour
½ teaspoon ground ginger
a little grated lemon rind
1 × 142 ml/5 fl oz carton double cream, whipped, (optional) with 1-2 tablespoons brandy added if liked

Preheat the oven to moderate, 180°C (350°F), Gas Mark 4. Combine the butter, sugar and syrup in a small saucepan and melt gently. Remove from the heat and stir in the flour, ginger and lemon rind. Cool.

Line a baking sheet with non-stick baking parchment. Drop two heaped teaspoons of the mixture on to the baking sheet, placing them well apart, then flatten them slightly. Bake for 7 to 8 minutes, until evenly browned.

Cool on the tray for 3 to 4 minutes, until the brandy snaps are cool enough to handle, then quickly wrap them around the oiled handle of a wooden spoon before sliding them off on to a wire rack to cool completely. If the brandy snaps harden before you manage to roll them up, pop them back into the oven for a minute or two to soften. Make more brandy snaps in the same way, using the same piece of non-stick parchment throughout. Serve the brandy snaps plain, or fill the ends with whipped cream, using a teaspoon or a piping bag fitted with a shell nozzle.

ROQUEFORT DIP

Pack this dip into an attractive pottery dish, cover with cling film or cellophane, tie a ribbon around and tuck a dried flower into the bow.

Serves 2
75 g/3 oz Roquefort cheese
225 g/8 oz cottage cheese
freshly ground black pepper

Break the Roquefort into pieces. Place in a blender or food processor with the cottage cheese and whizz to a purée. Season with freshly ground black pepper and transfer to a small dish to serve, with oatcakes or other savoury biscuits.

H I N T S   A N D   T I P S

Healthy Eating

For maximum health and vitality, all signs of the Zodiac should choose a diet high in fresh fruit and vegetables, with plenty of complex carbohydrates, proteins and small quantities of fats. Include grains, preferably whole, such as brown rice, plus wholemeal bread, potatoes, pasta and pulses.

An easy way to achieve this is to substitute skimmed or semi-skimmed milk for whole milk; to make breakfast a low-fat meal and to base one other meal of the day upon vegetables, fruits or grains.

A suitable breakfast might be one of the following:

- Fruit juice and toast with a scraping of butter or margarine and honey or marmalade

- Porridge made with water and served with skimmed milk or Greek yogurt

- Plain thick yogurt with fresh fruit

- Wholegrain sugar-free muesli with skimmed or semi-skimmed milk or fresh fruit juice

- Fresh fruit compote

The vegetable, fruit or grain-based meal might be:

- Florida Salad (page 135)

- Potato and Onion Soup (page 55) or other home-made soup, with a crusty wholewheat roll

- Chinese-style Stir-fried Vegetables (page 85)

- Baked potatoes filled with cottage cheese

- Wholemeal sandwiches with the minimum of butter or low-fat spread and lots of fresh lettuce, sliced tomato, cress, cucumber, perhaps some grated carrot and a slice or two of avocado. A little mayonnaise or low-calorie salad cream may be added.

When planning the main meal of the day, try to achieve a good nutritional balance. Serve a main course which contains fat (such as quiche), accompanied by lightly steamed vegetables without butter or rich sauces, or a salad, and add a low-fat dessert.

COOKING BROWN RICE

Brown rice is easy to cook as long as you give it enough time! For 4 portions, use the following foolproof method.

Spoon sufficient brown rice into a measuring jug to fill to the 300 ml/10 fl oz mark. Put the rice in a heavy-bottomed saucepan with 2-3 measures of water (600-900 ml/1-1½ pints). Use 2 measures if you want drier, more chewy rice, 2½-3 measures for softer rice that holds together well, good for serving with a stir fry, especially if it is to be eaten with chopsticks! Add 1 teaspoon salt (if liked), bring to the boil, then cover the pan tightly, turn the heat right down and simmer undisturbed for 45 minutes. By this time all the water should have been absorbed. If not, remove the pan from the heat and leave to stand, still covered, for a further 10-15 minutes. Fluff up the rice by forking it.

MAKING WHOLEMEAL PASTRY

Some people shy away from wholemeal pastry, claiming it is tough and heavy. This is a pity because it is not only healthier than white pastry, thanks to the natural bran contained in the flour, but also has a delicious nutty taste. Because wholemeal flour is less starchy than white flour, the pastry does not hold together so well and may require a little more water. Be careful not to add too much liquid, however, or you will end up with a very hard, heavy result.

I find the right proportions are, in metric measurements, 200 g wholemeal flour with 100 g butter or polyunsaturated vegetable margarine and 30-45 ml water; in imperial measures, 8 oz wholemeal flour, 4 oz butter or polyunsaturated margarine and 3 tablespoons water.

I must admit that I hardly ever chill pastry after making it, but roll it straight out, and the results are fine. It is easiest to roll the pastry out on a lightly floured board and then slide it straight off into the flan dish or pie plate. Alternatively, roll it over the rolling pin, lift and place it in position over the baking dish, then unroll. Avoid trying to lift pastry unsupported or it may tear. Bake in the usual way or as described in this book.

MAKING BREAD

In my experience the two most important tips for successful breadmaking are to make sure that the yeast you are using is really fresh, and to see that the mixture does not at any time get too hot before going into the oven. Fresh yeast should be pale beige in colour, springy and break easily into flaky pieces; it should smell fresh and pleasant.

If you use dried yeast or easy-blend yeast, make sure it is well within the use-by-date and has been stored in a cool, dry place. If dried yeast fails to froth up to a good head – like that on a glass of beer – or if it smells 'winey' after dissolving in water, throw it away and buy some more because it will not work.

When dissolving dried yeast, do not have the water hotter than hand-hot. Yeast is killed by heat, but not by cold; coldness just slows up the rising process. Put the bread dough in a warm place to rise. A draught-free corner close to (but not touching) a radiator is ideal. Equally good is an airing cupboard, if you have one. If you want the dough to rise more slowly, let it stand, covered with a clean, damp cloth, at room temperature. The slower the rise, the better the bread.

MAKING PRESERVES

The fruit should be firm and a bit underripe if possible. A large saucepan may be used, but a preserving pan is best if you are keen on making preserves.

Before you begin, wash and dry the jam jars and put them into a preheated cool oven, 150°C (300°F), Gas Mark 2, to sterilize and heat them at the same time. Never add hot preserve to cold jars – they may crack.

After adding the sugar to the cooked fruit or vegetables, make sure that it is completely dissolved before bringing the mixture to the boil.

To test for a set, put a little of the preserve on to a chilled saucer, chill for a couple of minutes, then push the surface of the preserve with a fingertip. If the preserve wrinkles, the mixture is ready. If not, boil vigorously for a further 3 minutes and test again.

When the setting point is reached, remove the preserve from the heat and stir in a knob of butter or margarine to disperse the scum. Allow the mixture to stand for 10 to 15 minutes for the fruit to settle (otherwise it will rise in the jars), then pour the mixture into the clean, warm jars. Cover immediately to avoid problems later with mould, but label the jars when they are cold or the labels will fall off!

CRYSTALLIZING FLOWERS

The flowers should be as perfect as possible, non-poisonous of course, and clean and dry. Whisk an egg white lightly, just to break it up, and add 1-2 teaspoons of water to thin it a little. Either dip the flower heads into the egg white, or paint the egg white carefully on to them using a fine paint brush. Dip the flowers in caster sugar, making sure they are completely coated. The flowers may be placed on non-stick baking parchment or waxed paper and left in a warm, dry place to dry, or they may be put into an oven on the lowest setting until they are completely dry. Store in an airtight tin.

INDEX

Editor Diana Craig
Art editors David Rowley, Lee Griffiths
Production controller Alyssum Ross
Copy editor Jenni Fleetwood
Designer Clive Hayball
Illustrations Nicholas Hely-Hutchinson
Photography James Murphy
Photographic styling Sarah Wiley
Preparation of food for photography Allyson Birch